THE ENTREPRENEUR'S SOULBOOK

PART I: IS IT YOUR CUP OF TEA?

SWATI JENA

INDIA • SINGAPORE • MALAYSIA

Notion Press

Old No. 38, New No. 6
McNichols Road, Chetpet
Chennai - 600 031

First Published by Notion Press 2019
Copyright © Swati Jena 2019
All Rights Reserved.

ISBN 978-1-64587-228-3

This book has been published with all efforts taken to make the material error-free after the consent of the author. However, the author and the publisher do not assume and hereby disclaim any liability to any party for any loss, damage, or disruption caused by errors or omissions, whether such errors or omissions result from negligence, accident, or any other cause.

No part of this book may be used, reproduced in any manner whatsoever without written permission from the author, except in the case of brief quotations embodied in critical articles and reviews.

Ma, Baba, Ruchi,
I will be nothing without you
Ujjwal,
I learnt many things about life and entrepreneurship from you.
You found the writer in me.

CONTENTS

Note from the Author		*7*
Chapter 1	Self-Awareness Before Product Idea	11
	◆ *Reflection guide for Chapter I*	*26*
Chapter 2	Why do you Want to Become an Entrepreneur?	31
	◆ *Reflection guide for Chapter II*	*55*
Chapter 3	Is Entrepreneurship Your Cup of Tea?	57
	◆ *Reflection guide for Chapter III*	*77*
Chapter 4	Family, Duties, Installments	79
	◆ *Reflection guide for Chapter IV*	*101*
Chapter 5	About Keeping a Side Job	105
	◆ *Reflection guide Chapter V*	*120*
Chapter 6	How Big a Business Should you Aspire to Build?	121

Chapter 7	Are you Ready to Take the Plunge?	133
	♦ *Reflection guide for Chapter VII*	*157*

NOTE FROM THE AUTHOR

It feels weird writing about yourself in the third person (though it makes you sound cool and important). I am going to write this in the first person.

I am Swati Jena, the author of this book.

I have lived the life of an entrepreneur twice. The first time I took the plunge; I took it simply on a hunch; and with none of the preparation I have described in this book.

It was really my phase of:

I don't know - that I don't know

I did not make many profits. I did not sink entirely. However, by the end of one year, I knew there was more preparation required.

After my first stint, I worked in an intrapreneurship-type product role within a large organization. I witnessed how a product is built, taken to market and scaled. More importantly, I experienced first-hand, how structure emerges from chaos in an entrepreneurial set-up; how there are days you think, "this is not going to work"; you feel like giving up. Yet, you need to get up and show up.

I was ready for my second stint. This time, it felt different.

I wrote this book realizing that all of the preparation we do for entrepreneurship is in terms of how to crack the business model, get funding, market the product, etc.

However, most entrepreneurs struggle due to reasons that are completely different from business issues. Entrepreneurs fail because they become too attached to their business idea to see its fault; because they become obsessed with growing too big too soon; because they succumb to fear; because they are unable to deal with pressure; or because they feel their family is not supportive. There are also many who have the potential to become good entrepreneurs but never get into entrepreneurship, because they keep waiting eternally for that one perfect idea or are too afraid to take the plunge.

This book sums up the many dilemmas of entrepreneurs right from the point they begin thinking about entrepreneurship:

Do I have it in me to become an entrepreneur?

Is it a foolish move to take a risk at this stage of my career?

Will I regret trying entrepreneurship - what if I fail?

Will I regret not trying entrepreneurship – what if I had tried?

How much money should I save? How should I convince my family? Who should I partner with? Should I keep a side job? Etcetera, etcetera.

The book is based on my personal reflection and interaction with several entrepreneurs at different stages of their journey spanning across:

- "Someday I want to be an entrepreneur."
- "I am an entrepreneur now."
- "I was an entrepreneur but it did not work out."
- "I am an entrepreneur and I made it big."

This is the first part of a series, where each part will explore the questions that keep entrepreneurs awake at night at different stages of the journey. This part begins at the beginning, where a person wonders whether entrepreneurship is really his cup of tea, and should he take the plunge.

If you are an aspiring entrepreneur reading this, I hope it helps you ask questions that will lead you to better prepare for your entrepreneurial stint. If you are reading it just out of curiosity, I hope you enjoy the read and find something useful anyway.

Either way, I hope it is worth your time.

P.S: All my pronouns in this book are masculine. That is only for ease of narration. I personally know of many wonderful women entrepreneurs. I am one of them. My wish and hope is to see their number increase. I am asked, every now and then, about the "challenges of a woman entrepreneur". My answer has always been that – an entrepreneur is an entrepreneur. The market doesn't differentiate between a man and woman. The customers don't expect anything less or more from you, based on your gender. You are just as accountable to your employees, investors and other stakeholders.

So don't get caught up with, he or she. Once you are an entrepreneur, you are just that.

This book is for every entrepreneur who, more than anything else, is committed to living life bravely, curiously and adventurously. Because, in the end, that is the only true spirit of entrepreneurship.

After reading this book, should you feel like reading more of what I write, you can find me on the following social handles:

- **Twitter:** swatcat_sj
- **Instagram:** swatcat_sj
- **Medium:** https://medium.com/@swati_jena
- **LinkedIn:** https://www.linkedin.com/in/swatijena/

As you will find in this book, I am an advocate of asking the right questions. My Tedx talk in 2018, is also about that. It's called, **Life is like a Google Screen,** delivered at **TedxYouth@SISMumbai**

https://www.youtube.com/watch?v=DKsHiWxiZuw

Chapter 1

SELF-AWARENESS BEFORE PRODUCT IDEA

I. Investment decisions are based on the entrepreneur, as much as the idea itself

In 2013, I had my first entrepreneurial stint. I started a training firm. I did that for a year. I earned enough to stay afloat, but I could not scale. I had a good idea. But I needed a team and partners to take it to the next level. Infact, I had a few offers from peers who were interested in joining as partners. But I, came in my own way.

I will tell you how, later.

Lot of entrepreneurship literature is dedicated to studying why any start-up becomes successful or fails. Firstly, all of that analysis happens in retrospect. It is easy to break down, critique, and provide reasons for something that has already happened. But, is there a way we can predict whether a start-up will be successful or not, in future?

In the world of VCs and funders, it is a known norm that a significant factor behind any funding decision is the entrepreneur himself. Investors bet on that, more than the idea itself. This is because, there is no way of saying whether a good idea will lead to a successful business. A good idea is just the beginning. All successful start-ups go through several rounds of changes to the idea itself, how it is executed, taken to customers, monetized, etc. All of those emerge with time.

The only concrete information initially, is the person behind the idea. Investors want to know, more than anything else, about the founder and his team. If you have had the opportunity to talk to, or read books by seasoned investors, you will find that they pay a lot of attention to this aspect. It appears that people, who bet their money on start-ups, try to predict the success of it, by assessing the entrepreneur.

II. Assessing an entrepreneur is important, but not easy

The unfortunate part of this process, is that often the assessment of a first-time entrepreneur gets based on potentially misleading criterion like pedigree; whether someone went to Wharton, IIT or MIT; is an ex-Google, ex-Apple.

While there is a lot of criticism of this pedigree-bias, perhaps we should cut the investors some slack. It is indeed an imperfect measure of an entrepreneur's ability and an even more inaccurate predictor of a start-up's success. However, assessing the deepest motivations, value system and characteristics of a person, is an HR nightmare. Even with a complete battery of psychometric tools developed over decades, it is nearly impossible to assess and predict human beings with certainty. One can only imagine the difficulty of gauging an entrepreneur across few hours of interaction. If that assessment would have been easy, then the business world would not be full of examples where entrepreneurs did not live up to their promise and top executives in corporates were found to be wrong fits for their roles - long after they were hired.

Because it is nearly impossible to gauge the inner workings of a human being during a short business pitch, many surface qualities like pedigree, communication and confidence tend to get considered. The assumption is, if someone went to a good school and worked for good organizations, then the:

a. Person has some capabilities

b. Person has a drive to achieve

c. Person has already been assessed by leading educational institutions and organizations, so there must be something right about this person

All of these could be faulty assumptions in many cases. What makes you successful in educational institutes and within the four walls of an organization could be very different from what is needed for success in entrepreneurship.

The moot point here is that, people who invest in start-ups, realize the importance of assessing the entrepreneur - whether or not, there are perfect ways of doing so.

III. Businesses fail more often due to personal reasons, than business reasons

A much-quoted statistic in the entrepreneurship world is that 9 out of 10 start-ups fail. That is a statistic worth thinking about. Why do so many ventures fail?

Analysts give a variety of reasons ranging from product not being unique, business model, competition, execution, differences between partners, cash burn out, etc. What manifests as business problems on the surface, are often deep-rooted person-related factors.

For example:

Consider a product or service idea that found no acceptance in the market.

A part of the reason could be market conditions. But what about aspects like; does the founder seek feedback (a) on time and (b) from the right people? Does he involve people in his product decisions? Does he involve too many people and the wrong ones? Or is he too much in love with his product idea to change it even when it is not working?

Consider a business that failed trying to scale up too much too soon.

Sometimes it could be an error of judgement, or things not going as planned. Many times, it could be the lack of planning itself. Is the entrepreneur in the game only to scale, make money and exit? Is the entrepreneur too rash to prepare, before taking the leap? Does the entrepreneur not care enough about customers and employees who suffer when there is unsustainable scale? Does the entrepreneur run after metrics that attract investment, instead of setting a strong foundation for sustainable long-term growth?

We can similarly look deeper into any supposed "business reason". Almost always we will find a whole lot of person related issues behind it. Mind you, I said person-issues not people-issues. They are slightly different. "People issues", usually refer to team dynamics, motivations, alignment to a vision, etc. When I say "person-issue", I am really referring, very specifically, to the beliefs, values and intentions of the entrepreneur himself.

Therefore, we can conclude that:

a. The inner workings of an entrepreneur's mind are mission critical; and

b. Assessing this accurately is very difficult from the outside, by outsiders

However, it is possible for entrepreneurs themselves to develop this understanding about their own minds; both, possible and essential. Therefore, an entrepreneurial journey cannot start with thinking of a business idea. It has to begin with thinking about oneself.

Infact let me suggest a radical idea:

> *The lack of self-awareness in an entrepreneur is a strong indicator of an imminent failure.*

An entrepreneur may have brilliant ideas and a good understanding of the market. However, if he has no understanding of himself, he may get lucky a few times; but he will eventually get stuck. Self-awareness can help an entrepreneur prepare and adapt better to everything that will come his way. Infact, self-awareness is a pre-requisite to building adaptability. And no entrepreneur can survive, without being adaptable.

Let me share an example. I know of an entrepreneur who is a very intelligent, well-read and someone who wants to create real value for customers. He is qualified to serve the customers given his education, experience and expertise in that field. However, he tends to become very stubborn on very inconsequential things – to the extent of it being a deal-breaker of some revenue generating business. His close friends are of the view that he might even be very proud of being headstrong.

The flaw in being this way might be obvious to many people. But it is not obvious to this entrepreneur. He is not self-aware in this matter. As a result of that, he is also unable to adapt to how a business needs to be run. Until he changes that one thing about him, a business might be difficult, despite all his other capabilities.

This is what I mean by saying – entrepreneurs MUST build self-awareness even before they start building a product.

Adaptability means change.

- How can you "change" something that you are "not aware" of?

- How can you adapt your style if you don't understand the inner working of your mind?

- How do you decide what to stand by and when to let go, if you are not clear about - what really matters to you, and what you can do without?

- What about partners and core employees? If you don't know your own strengths, weaknesses, triggers, values – how will you select the right combination of people?

I don't even need to provide statistics on the just-too-many partnership failures that happen in the entrepreneurial world.

That brings me to that story I began with.

IV. We always over-estimate how much we know ourselves

I mentioned at the beginning of the chapter, that I could not scale up my first entrepreneurial venture – because I came in my own way. Let me tell you about it now.

In 2013, I could not take on more partners because I had so many questions in my mind about the intent, capability and compatibility of any partners who would come on board. I felt very uncomfortable parting with what I had built. I even felt I wasn't being loyal to my idea – by sharing it with someone else.

I am sure the flaw in that line of thinking appears very obvious. But it wasn't obvious to me at that time. It wasn't until 2016, when I was far removed from that situation that I could look back at the situation from a distance. It was then that I realized, that the discomfort I experienced in 2013 was actually a lack of trust. Also, that I was making the mistake of trying to find someone "like me", instead of someone who complimented me.

This episode taught to me two things.

- **Learning #1: No matter how many books you read or advice you receive, none of that is a substitute of self-awareness**

Until you can see it in yourself, merely knowing something intellectually does not ensure you will not make a mistake. Had that been the case, no entrepreneur or human being would make the mistakes already made by millions in the past. That is just the nature of human beings. We may read books, listen to others' experiences, watch videos; yet we make so many mistakes of our own.

Even in my case, I had read that you should find a business partner who compliments you, instead of being similar to you. But that did not prevent me from making the very same mistake on-ground. This was because, it was not enough to just know the concept in my head. I needed the ability to feel trust in another person. So, knowledge cannot help you beyond a point. But, awareness can.

I am aware today about how my mind works around trust. So, I operate differently, and am actually able to trust more. Self-awareness helped me, not books.

> *In matters of changing oneself, the only way out is to look within.*

- **Learning #2: We always, grossly overestimate how much we know ourselves**

Ask anyone around, or, even your own self: "how much do you think you know yourself". Most of us, are likely to respond that we know ourselves fairly well. Infact, we feel offended if someone tries to tell us anything about us. Worst, we never seek feedback about ourselves.

If you ask me how much I know myself, I will say with all the confidence in the world – "pretty darn well". I spend a lot of time introspecting since childhood. I have intuitively known the importance of being self-aware very early in my life. And while those are factually correct, I never realized how much I did not know about myself. They say the lowest form of ignorance is:

> *I don't know, that I don't know.*

As human beings, when it comes to self-awareness, we are all vulnerable to this level of ignorance. We spend our entire lives acquiring knowledge in schools and colleges to prepare for jobs. While on jobs we acquire knowledge to prepare for promotions. No part of growing up – or grown-up life is dedicated to reflecting about oneself. Until some life-shattering event happens, someone is lying on the hospital bed with a heart-attack, losing someone or something they value – this exercise on self-awareness never features on the priority list.

But we have to start somewhere. So, here is an idea.

V. Start with a vacation

When people are planning to start off as entrepreneurs, there is a lot of external and self-imposed pressure to get started soon; to decide on an idea; to be fast. If you have quit your job, you will count every month that goes past without you launching your business.

If you are coming out of a sabbatical, you are likely to think that you have been "doing nothing" for a long time and must get started now. You will be under self-imposed pressure of coming up with something fast. Yet, you should consider going off to some place you can be alone for a while. Do it, even if you were on a so-called break till now. Go someplace quiet and calm, close to nature if possible. Leave behind people and gadgets. Spend time with yourself. Don't do sightseeing, trekking, marathon practice, mediation.

Don't to be in a hurry to find answers.

Your only objective is to create emptiness and space within yourself, and immerse yourself in questions. If you are a Type A (hyper-active, over-working) personality, this may be difficult; but that is all the more reason you should do it. So, here is what I am saying.

> *Forget about product idea. Start your entrepreneurial journey by going on a holiday…with yourself.*

Reflection guide for Chapter I

Pre-entrepreneurship vacation reflection

Instruction: The following questions will help you focus on some of the key qualities an entrepreneur needs to have. Be honest with yourself. Think of how you have actually behaved in the near past, and not how you think you are. These are not either-you-are-either-you-are-not type of answers. You might be good or bad at them in varying degrees. The awareness is meant to help you pre-empt your potential failure – and work on them proactively.

Also, purchase a new diary and write down your answers. Revisiting these pages in the future can be more helpful than you can imagine at this point in time.

1. **How self-driven are you?**

    See if you can find atleast 3 occasions in the last 3 years, where you have taken up and completed something on your own, i.e. not because of some professional requirement or someone in the family coaxed you. It should be something that needed some bit of persistence; i.e. not like a 1- or 2-day photography class – but say a 3-month French course, or setting up your own blogspot and writing on it regularly

2. **How focused are you?**

    Focus is the ability to give all your attention to your most important goals, despite distractions, detractors, and any other mess-up going on around you. Look back into your life and find atleast one or two significant goals you achieved by staying focused even when there were many other things calling for your attention.

3. How disciplined are you?

How often do people have to follow-up with you for completion of work? Are you the kind who has to be given a wake-up call in the morning? Do you do things last moment? Are you always running late to meetings? Do you have control over how you eat, sleep, exercise? Do you watch TV and videos mindlessly? Etc. etc. This are good cues to how disciplined you are.

4. How do you respond to stress?

Do you start binging? Lose your cool? Take it out on family? Get demotivated? Also, what triggers stress? How long does the stress response last? How do you come out of it (if you do)? Make a log of your last 10 stress situations and answer these questions about each of them.

5. How do you take decisions?

Do you consciously list the criterion you take decisions on? E.g. if you are thinking – "will this make me popular" – then "fame" is your criterion. If you thought "this will make my parents proud in society" – then "validation/social approval" was your criterion. At this stage the question is not whether a criterion is good or bad. The question you are answering is – whether you consciously choose that criterion and assign a priority to it (or take decisions without conscious awareness of these?)

Secondly, how do you select the people you consult for a decision? Are they the same set of friends, mentors, colleagues who you are comfortable with? Or do you consciously evaluate if someone will be able to give you good advice on a certain matter?

Thirdly, do you take their advice at face value? Or do you ask them in-depth questions? Do you evaluate why they are giving the advice they are – and if it is good for you?

6. How do you feel about smarter people, at peer-level or junior to you?

Do you like to be the smartest person in the room? Or are you comfortable with people who know things better than you? How do you feel about such people? Are you comfortable letting them function the way they want to or do you feel the need to control them? Think back in your life, whether work or education – did you put yourself in groups where the capability of people was the same as, or less than you – or did you actively work with people who were better than you?

7. **How is your ability to let go of things that are dear to you?**

   Can you come up with atleast 5 examples in the last 3-5 years when you have let go (willingly) of something that you were very attached to – a thing, a person, an idea, a point of view? How open you are to listening to a different point of view on a matter you feel strongly about? How strong is your attachment to physical things – because they have a sentimental value, psychological value, societal value, etc.

Chapter 2

WHY DO YOU WANT TO BECOME AN ENTREPRENEUR?

I. Why the 'why' matters

"Are you looking to become an entrepreneur per se, or you would be okay even if you got an exciting job at this stage?" I asked my friend.

Many friends from the professional world I know are those who:

- Already were or are entrepreneurs
- Are thinking of becoming an entrepreneur in the future
- Are not thinking of entrepreneurship but wondering if anything is wrong with them for not aspiring to be an entrepreneur (like every other person)

The category of "thinking of becoming an entrepreneur" is particularly crowded; which is why I end up having these why-do-you-want-to-become-an-entrepreneur discussions often. I hear several interesting phrases, during those discussions. The most common one being, "I want to do something of my own".

Now, that is a loaded phrase. It needs unpeeling to get to the heart of what it really means. I suspect that often people use this phrase not knowing what they exactly mean by it. Across many such conversations, I have come to understand that this single phrase refers to a whole variety of things:

- "I want to do something of my own. I am tired of this 9 to 5."
- "I want to do something of my own. I want to be my own boss."

- "I want to do something of my own. I want to do something big."
- "I want to do something of my own. I want have my own identity."

While some are seeking greater control over their time, others are looking for power to decide what work they do and how they do it. Some want to utilize their capabilities more, while others want to stand out in the crowd. There are many in search of the proverbial pot of gold in shape of a million-dollar start-up idea they can build and sell - and live happily ever after.

It also appears that often a job that is boring, tiring, limiting, meaningless, debilitating and life-sucking, or any combination of those, is behind many professionals fantasizing about entrepreneurship. The need to get oneself out of such a job is understandable. But to think that entrepreneurship is your way out - is a problematic approach.

> *Trying to become an entrepreneur under the false assumption*
>
> *that it has none of the miseries of a regular job*
>
> *is like setting oneself up*
>
> *for a bad marriage burdened with unrealistic expectations.*

Entrepreneurship is not like a holiday or haircut that provides respite from the drudgery of daily life. Entrepreneurship is a high-stake game. Unless you have inherited some ancestral fortune, for a normal working person, just one year spent to start a business means:

- The opportunity cost of what you would have earned on a job that year
- Savings used up to manage expenses for that year and initial business investment
- Loss of a year of experience in a specific domain, and the need to explain a break (that's how HR is likely to see this stint, should you choose to go back to work)

For youngsters, just out of college, this has consequences too:

- Continuing to live off your parents' money (this is particularly troublesome if you belong to a middle or lower income family, where your parents have taken a student loan to finance your studies and you have siblings in the pipeline)
- Finding a job if your venture fails (statistics say, you will most likely fail in your first attempt – HR is usually confused with what to do with your kind of profiles)

So, if you are either very rich, or have not built anything worth losing, then I guess you can go about entrepreneurship in any way you wish. But for the larger number of people in-between, it is necessary to think this through well.

> *I am not making this point to discourage you from entrepreneurship.*
> *I am making this point to encourage you, to do it, for the right reasons.*

In life, there are two kinds of reasons we do anything for – good reasons and bad reasons. Entrepreneurship is no different. There are people who choose entrepreneurship for good reasons, and there are those who choose it for the bad ones. It is important to be aware which one is driving you.

Here are some of the good and bad reasons behind anyone becoming an entrepreneur.

II. Top bad reasons to become an entrepreneur

One common thread across all the bad reasons is that they treat entrepreneurship as either a short-cut to achieve something or provide an escape from something. Bad reasons arise, from a superficial understanding of one's problems, to which entrepreneurship is wrongly assumed to be the solution.

- **Bad reason #1: I want to make (quick) millions**

There is nothing wrong with wanting to make millions. But there is everything wrong about that being the central driving force of doing anything in life, including choosing a profession. If someone starts his entrepreneurial journey with, making-loads-of-money as the key driver, things are bound to get very difficult in future. Following are just few of the many things an entrepreneur ends up doing wrong, if his ambition is to make big bucks quickly.

Short-sighted product decisions: Entrepreneurs who are in the game to make quick money, are very vulnerable to taking short-sighted product decisions. Their focus is quick scale-and-sale, and not laying a strong foundation to the product. For example, they are very likely to not spend enough time in research during the initial stages of the product development. They may not spend enough time evaluating features, platforms, doing enough pilots or running quality checks. The focus is always to get the product off the ground and rush into sales.

Unsustainable offers to customers: This is a known phenomenon, especially in many ecommerce-based businesses. In a bid to scale up fast, many freebies are offered to entice the customers. Often, these cannot be sustained by the business plan. Features are offered, with no budget for upgrades in future. Often there are fine prints, and difficult exit clauses. Overall, it a complete set-up leading the customer to feel frustrated and deceived in the end.

No business plan to build service excellence: How you deliver products to customers, is as important as, building a good product. It is observed widely, that organizations miss out on planning for service delivery until it is too late. Hiring is done in a haste, getting the wrong people on board. Customers are left feeling frustrated. I wrote a blog on this subject on LinkedIn, which resonated with many professionals. It was titled:

"Who pays the price?": Why innovative products without service excellence hurt customers – the ethics of product innovation

The core essence of the article was that the real validation of a brilliant product is successfully delivering the promise which was sold to the customer. It is not "sales numbers", which is often show-cased. People in business and corporates know how numbers can be engineered. An entrepreneur, who is driven by just money, will attempt to build scale on an unsustainable basis, which will finally hurt employees in form of sudden layoffs, unrealistic work pressures and disappoint customers with poor service.

It finally also hurts those who buy-off or acquire that venture. Corporate world is full of examples where companies acquire start-ups only to realize (alas, too late), that they got carried away by the scale. The scale was built on unsustainable business models and promises; and the customers start disappearing sooner than the acquiring company can get their act together.

I read somewhere an article on the fabulous life of Evan Spiegel, the Snapchat founder. A part of the article focused on his journey that led to Snapchat and how it progressed from there. The other part of the article focused on his fabulous life – the billions, the cars, the magazine cover pages, the mansions, etc. There are many such articles about billionaires who built-a-business-and-became-rich. The question an aspiring entrepreneur should ask oneself is – exactly which part of those stories does he find himself influenced by? Is it the thrill of building the product, the struggle and journey or just the glitz and glamour?

Having done the soul-searching, if indeed you find that your mind is attracted mostly by the glamour, you should consider staying away from entrepreneurship. You rarely ever succeed in entrepreneurship the very first time. It often involves a lot of hard work, risk, decisions, and things not going as per plan. If glory is the only thing you are running after, you will be down and out in no time. Unless you have some inheritance to fall back on, you may even be struggling to keep your head above water.

Don't get into entrepreneurship if you are not prepared for all the hard stuff.

- **Bad reason #2: "I was better than him in college. If he can do it, I can too"**

Often, we get carried away by what we see on the surface. And success, as displayed on social media, has a particularly strong ability to blind us. When we get to know about an ex-colleague who has become successful in entrepreneurship, or a college senior or someone in the family, it gives rise to thoughts of, "if he can do it, I can do it too".

But it doesn't work that way. Firstly, we might be getting carried away by surface information. I know of many cases when a general perception of a business doing well gets built based on social media marketing, a few event updates, interview of the entrepreneur in some online magazine. I am a second-time entrepreneur, and I can tell you that these small wins are a huge morale boost for the entrepreneur and his team. I will also tell you that these are not enough to call a business successful. Even if you have received funding, your business cannot be called successful. Speaking at events, getting noticed on social media, getting funded may show potential for success, but it is not success itself. Unless a business has sustained growth with profit for a few years, a business is not successful.

And if you, as a would-be entrepreneur, are to base your decision on things that don't reflect real success, you are creating trouble for yourself. Because when you enter the business inspired by these superfluous measures, you will consciously or unconsciously focus on the wrong goals. Being noticed on social media, getting interviewed or winning awards are a real high for any entrepreneur. But I will say again, the goal and measure of a successful business is to make sustained profits by creating products that add some real value to the customer.

There is another aspect of this "if he can do it, I can do it too" mindset. Sometimes it comes from comparing oneself with that other person. "I am better educated than that person" or "I was a better student than him" or "he used to be this person with such low confidence". It is risky to make those comparisons.

That person may have become successful because of a whole lot of struggle, tough choices, taking risk and showing courage. A common human tendency is to compare, sort and rank people in our head for a lifetime - using parameters which may have been relevant decades ago, but are redundant now. A very simple example is how we perceive classmates and colleagues based on their exam grades or workplace performance ratings.

For example, say for a management degree you were the batch topper and there is one classmate, who was in the bottom rung of the class. Obviously, you were more successful and promising back then, and chances are you bagged a better job during campus placement. In another example, say you have joined a firm, and with a combination of your hard work, and some bit of luck on getting good assignments, and your skill for being in the good books of people in authority, you got high ratings for two years. In the same duration, there was this colleague who may not have done as well as you, or was not in the good books of people.

In both these scenarios, you are likely to place yourself as superior in your mind, than that other person, and form negative perceptions about the person's ability, intelligence, etc. Ten years later, you get know that this other person has become a successful entrepreneur. What are the chances, you are likely to think, "if he can do it, I can do it too"? Very high.

Many people suffer from this manner of thinking. What they don't realize is, for every game, the rules are different. The skills required for entrepreneurship are not the same as those required for getting the highest grades or becoming a good employee. The reason the guy who was at the bottom of the class, or not a blue-eyed-boy at work, became successful could be because he has a greater risk appetite, maybe he cares more for an idea than you do, he is more resourceful than you are, etc. Getting into entrepreneurship thinking, someone you considered less capable than you, has become successful - and by logical extension - that ensures your success, is a recipe for failure.

Just because someone can float well in a bath tub, does not mean he can swim in the high seas. And entrepreneurship is quite the high sea.

- **Bad reason #3: I am stuck in a bad job**

Let me begin with discussing the circumstances that make us take up jobs which feel suffocating. Following is why we end up this way.

Many of us continue to take jobs in areas we chose as our first careers. But the choice of a first career is nothing short of guess-work. Our first careers are based on grand assumptions our parents make, about what jobs are best for us; or our own perceptions, based on the career-choice of some random cousin, neighbour or senior.

Many of us choose professions that give the best guarantee of a well-paying job. It is often as straight-forward as that. Study this course and you will get a "sure-shot job". The race for top-tier colleges, is mostly for this reason.

The job pays bills, gets us respect as an earning member of the family and society. Slowly we start buying furniture, home, a car, get married, have kids and put them in school. Without realizing we build an entire life around a job which has nothing to do with our interests, talents, strengths or values.

One fine day, we start feeling stuck with a 9-to-5, and start fantasizing about entrepreneurship. And this is why it is a bad reason to become an entrepreneur.

> *9 to 5 is not the culprit.*
> *What you are doing between 9 and 5, is the real problem.*

I started this chapter with a conversation I was having with a friend of mine. He has been thinking of entrepreneurship for a while. Further into the conversation I learnt that he was very unhappy with the current job, which is when I asked him if he was clear about wanting to be an entrepreneur; or hypothetically if he got an exciting job offer, he would be happy with it.

It is a good question to ask oneself, if you seem to be driven by a current "bad job". Are you are really looking to become an entrepreneur or just seeking a desperate escape from an existing job? If latter, then you may be better off evaluating a change in job, taking a break or finding a completely new profession, by reskilling yourself, getting a new qualification. Don't worry about having to restart a few levels lower in a new profession (e.g. say you were in marketing and you want to get into product management). It is going to be worse in entrepreneurship. You may have a "CEO" written on the visiting card, but when you start off, you are essentially a salary-less guy who will even need to photo-copy the documents himself.

> *Opting for a 5-to-9 to escape a 9-to-5, with no other motivation driving you, is plain foolish, if the point was not already obvious.*

- **Bad reason #4: I am tired of this 9 to 5**

This reason is different from the previous one. "I am tired of this 9 to 5" indicates monotony in professional, and most likely personal life too. Often, we get so caught up in the rat race that we neglect investing in other aspects of our life. Once upon a time we used to have a thing called hobby. It is nearly extinct these days. The only other things we seem to be doing apart from going to work is watching TV, movies and visiting the mall. Families cannot have a decent conversation together; let alone doing joint activities and genuinely enjoying each other's company.

We have stopped tapping into our own selves to keep alive that one thing that excited us when we were kids – maybe gardening, some form of craft, jamming with friends. We also invest very little in keeping our professional lives exciting. And this is despite spending many hours at work. Sitting at your desk 14 hours a day is not equal to taking real interest in your profession. How many professionals really spend time learning about things beyond their immediate job, create something in their own profession, read up or write about it?

Slowly life becomes this routine of the 9 to 5.

Entrepreneurship looks like a shiny, glamorous and exciting life from a distance that will rescue you from boredom. If you are not capable of creating excitement in your existing life, you will make a mess of your entrepreneurial life aswell. If you think entrepreneurship is always fun and does not include plain and dull work, that is as far from truth as you can get.

A word for freshers here too. While freshers don't have the baggage of a first career to run away from, freshers can suffer from the same misgivings as working professionals. They too can be fooled into thinking that entrepreneurship has none of the drudgery of a regular job. Entrepreneurship can be even more tedious and you may not find the guidance and cushion you have in a regular job. So, if you decide to become an entrepreneur, discard any notions of entrepreneurship being glamourous and shiny, in the nearest garbage bin you can find.

III. Top good reasons to become an entrepreneur

A common thread across all the "good reasons" is that they help the entrepreneur expand his potential in some way. Good reasons focus on something intrinsic rather than an external goal. Good reasons are also more honest and devoid of false perceptions that drive some of the bad reasons we discussed earlier.

Lot of entrepreneurship literature seems to be advocating the perception that all entrepreneurs necessarily begin their journey from wanting to solve a problem. I don't agree with it. That may be one of the starting places, but it is not the only one. Ofcourse, the product that the entrepreneur builds, has to ultimately solve some real problem. But the "desire to solve a problem" is not the only birthplace of all entrepreneurial endeavors. Here are some other very good reasons to become an entrepreneur.

- **Good reason #1: My ideal job does not exist**

I love this TV show called, Sherlock. When Watson and Sherlock Holmes meet in the beginning, Watson asks Holmes about his profession, who famously replies,

"I am a consulting detective. The only one in the world. I invented the job."

Sometimes you have to be like Sherlock Holmes, and invent your job role. And sometimes that means becoming an entrepreneur.

Corporations can be very limiting that way. Employees may work a greater number of hours, but they function at a lower level of potential. If you are some Director, you might be spending your time sitting in meetings, making presentations, planning visits of senior management, and trouble-shooting; all of these, instead of spending real time in thinking about the future product, process improvement and building the next level of leaders. Since the Director is doing the work of a General Manager who reports to him, the General Manager himself is pushed to work a few levels below his potential; and so on.

Asking for a higher level of work is considered blasphemy, and you are expected to wait for your turn to come. In years of careers in large corporations, most people have some phases of exciting work, but largely it is the same old routine. The corporate legend of Monday morning blues is perhaps an indication of this phenomenon.

Most people accept the status quo, rationalizing it with reasons such as EMIs, bills, responsibilities, etc. But there is a small set of people, who find it difficult to live with the feeling that they are capable of a lot more than they are doing currently.

If you belong to the second category, and think entrepreneurship might be your answer, you could be on the right track. One thing guaranteed about being an entrepreneur is that your boundaries and potential will be pushed to the maximum possible limit. You will learn by the day, discover things about yourself, and get exposure to areas outside your immediate professional expertise. So, if you are a person who wants to do much more than your workplace will ever allow you to - and you want to become an entrepreneur for that reason - I will say it is a pretty good reason.

- **Good reason #2: I am thrilled by the prospect of building something**

We might want to build something for many reasons. The first is the obvious reason of solving some problem, where the entrepreneur is attempting to do one of the following:

1. Build something for a problem with no existing solution
2. Build something for a problem which has a solution already – but yours is either a better solution or a different solution which is equally good

It is possible you will receive advice that if a problem already has a good solution, it is not worth spending time and money to find another one. I like something that author Elizabeth Gilbert wrote in her amazing book on creativity, Big Magic. She says:

> *Most things have already been done – but they have not yet been done by you.*

So, if you know you will be able to find customers, and your heart says you will build something unique even if there are other players in that field, go right ahead; even if it is the millionth bakery in the world, but you know there is going to be something special about your bread;

and customers will be willing to pay for it; please build your bakery or coffee shop or school or services - whatever it is that you dream of.

The second reason for an entrepreneur to build something is not connected to solving problems. I wonder what problem Walt Disney was trying to solve when he set out to lay the foundations of all-things-Disney. Sometimes the urge to build comes from place of pure creativity and imagination. What you create may end up solving some problem, or making something better – but your deepest drive comes from just the need to create. This is true for artists, scientists and entrepreneurs.

It is said about product development that you may build something with a certain use in mind, but customers may put it to an altogether different use. If you are inspired with just the deep desire to create something, go right ahead. Customers will find a use for it. You will think of something along the way.

- **Good reason #3: "I want to create my own legacy"**

I have met entrepreneurs whose reason for entrepreneurship is to create something that stays on, long after they are gone. Is it possible to create a legacy while being employed in an organization? Maybe yes, if you manage to reach the top of the ladder.

Maybe. A big maybe.

Creating a legacy is different from creating a name for yourself, or creating an impact with your work. Legacy is something that stays in form of practices, values and other such invisible things for a long time after the person is gone. Jamshedji Tata created a legacy. Dhirubhai Ambani created a legacy. Steve Jobs created a legacy.

And all of them were entrepreneurs.

Legacy is not about a product. It is not about an iPhone. Products change with technology. Who knows, we may not even have phones in future. Legacy is about beliefs. "People, who are crazy enough to think they can change the world, are the ones who actually do" is a belief. Mind you, it is not just a tag-line. It is what people live by. That is legacy. That will stay, whether or not iPhones do. What are the chances a hired CEO can leave behind a legacy in an organization which changes hands, changes leaders, gets acquired, and a whole lot of things?

> *An organizational role may offer you the opportunity to become a legend.*
>
> *But it seldom offers anyone the opportunity to leave behind a legacy.*

Only entrepreneurship can give you that. That is why this is a good reason.

- **Good reason #4: I just want to explore if I am made for this**

"I want to explore" is not the same "I want to try my luck".

Exploration requires commitment to turn every rock, venture on untrodden path, and go beyond your fears. Trying your luck is non-committal. It is like, let me buy a lottery ticket and see if I hit jackpot. It is like, let me tag along with this business partner and see if I can make it big ("what if this company gets sold for millions" type of a thought). Such a person will never show courage, enterprise or sweat – all of which are mission-critical to entrepreneurship.

A genuine interest to explore entrepreneurship is different, and is a great reason to become an entrepreneur. Infact, I will go a step further and say that, every professional must take a sabbatical to explore entrepreneurship atleast once in their life.

Entrepreneurship teaches you complete accountability, in a way a regular job never can – no matter how fantastic that job is. You cannot survive entrepreneurship unless you are self-driven. You have to learn multiple skills. You are the CEO and the peon, and everything else in between. Even if your venture fails, but you have given it your 100%, the learning is invaluable. I will hire such a person any day, over an organizational good performer.

IV. Finally, how do you find your reason?

Remember the first chapter, where we said you must start your journey with a holiday? "Why do I want to become an entrepreneur", is one of the key aspects to explore during that reflection. It is not going to be easy. The mind will lie to you, trick you, and give excuses. But you must be willing to be brutally honest with yourself.

Give yourself alternatives to entrepreneurship – and see if those alternatives make you happy.

What if you had a great manager...

What if you were doing fantastic in your work...

What if you had a great work environment...

Would you be happy doing a regular job?

If the answer is yes, then entrepreneurship is probably not what you really want.

You are only seeking an escape from your current circumstances.

But if you feel "something is missing" despite everything else being in place, then maybe you are really seeking entrepreneurship.

Now that you have figured out your "good reason", there is the next BIG question to ask...

(Before we explore that big question in the next chapter, use the reflection guide on the next page to find out what is driving you towards entrepreneurship)

Reflection guide for Chapter II

Finding your 'why' of entrepreneurship

I strongly recommend you write down the answers to these questions. You will be surprised to see what you have written down and the assumption you may have been making.

1. What about becoming an entrepreneur excites you?
2. How do you know, what you know about entrepreneurship (in other words, all the perceptions/assumptions you have about the entrepreneurial life – how did you build those perceptions? Write down the names of people you have read about, spoken to, etc)
3. Evaluate the above sources and write down if your perceptions are based on a broad variety of sources or biased by few individuals? Is your understanding of the entrepreneurial life realistic? This will help you understand if you have a strong basis for your entrepreneurial decision.
4. Of the good and bad reasons discussed in this chapter, which ones are driving you?

(Questions 6 to 10 are for professionals who have/had a corporate job)

5. Are you running away from your current job or fear/detest joining back the corporate world?
6. What do you not like about your job(s)?
7. Can those problems (#6) be solved if you got a different job/manager/new career?

8. Have you assumed you will not find those problems in entrepreneurship as well?
9. What do you like about your regular job(s)? Will you find those in entrepreneurship? If not, how will you manage?

Chapter 3

IS ENTREPRENEURSHIP YOUR CUP OF TEA?

I. The million-dollar question

"Is entrepreneurship my cup of tea?"

I suspect every person on the entrepreneurial journey asks himself this question at some point in time. But at what stage they ask this question, may vary from entrepreneur to entrepreneur. Often this question pops up in the mind when the going gets tough, and self-doubt creeps in. "Am I really made for this?" "Is all this hassle really my cup of tea?"

> *It is a strange habit of human beings to starting wondering about "why"*
> *when things go wrong, but not when it is a smooth sailing*

If an entrepreneur becomes successful because of other partners, or favorable conditions, i.e. he just gets lucky, he does not pause to ask – "do I have it in me?" But if things go downside, these existential questions become very loud inside the head.

> *The best time to think deeply about "why entrepreneurship" is neither when things are good nor bad. The best time is right at the beginning of the entrepreneurial journey.*

This question does not have an easy "yes" or "no" answer. There are those people who know very clearly that they are born to be entrepreneurs. And then there are those who just don't have it in them. But for the larger majority, it is a process of experimentation and discovery as they go along. Hence, it is important to keep revisiting this question during the journey.

Entrepreneurship is a continuum. The enterprising neighborhood lady turning her skill for cooking into a local business is an entrepreneur; and so is the big-shot hotelier with 5-star resorts around the world. Both have similarities, and yet are different in their thought, risk-taking abilities, value system, etc.

Hence, the question of "am I cut out for entrepreneurship" is not an easy one, nor does it have straight-forward answers. Maybe someone begins with thinking he will set up something small, and be happy. But along the way he realizes, he is actually capable of a lot more. It may be the other way around too. Therefore, I cannot emphasize more on the importance of asking this question continuously. Being honest to oneself, about one's real capabilities and aspirations, is very important for an entrepreneur. We cannot create anything valuable based on other's expectations of us, or their perception of our capability.

There are definitely a few qualities that differentiate a real entrepreneur from others who have lost their way into entrepreneurship. A good way to find out is to reflect on one's professional and personal life for critical incidents that may give some evidence of our entrepreneurial qualities.

Many would-be entrepreneurs focus their energy on learning entrepreneurial skills and knowledge. They try to master things like social media marketing, raising funds, type of legal entity, business model, etc. All of those are important. But all of them come second, and can be learnt along the way. What comes first is the understanding of entrepreneurial attitudes and values. So, when I talk about reflecting on qualities of a real entrepreneur, I am talking about attitudes and values.

The thing with attitudes and values is that they are developed over several years through our unique life experiences. They are deep-seated and also relatively difficult to change. Thus, an entrepreneur must explore and discover if he has those attitudes.

The following are some cues to answering if someone has it in him to be an entrepreneur.

II. Hints to whether you are the entrepreneur type

- **Hint#1: Are you the FORMULA guy?**

We start looking for these early in life, perhaps at school. It is known by different names; formulas, tricks, techniques and hacks. If you apply them in a certain systematic way, it will lead to a predictable result; acing tests, cracking interviews, managing your boss, winning a girl, building your brand. Bad news is that formulas may work in a few cases. But for things that really matter, life seldom plays out within any formula.

The unfortunate thing is most people, take formulas at face value. They do not care to understand the underlying context and assumptions. Infact, the very reason many people seek formulas is that they don't want to break their head, and hope they can make it big, with minimal efforts. If you belong to this category, you probably keep reading articles, taking expert advice with the objective of finding a fool-proof way of becoming successful. Bad news is that entrepreneurship may not be your cup of tea.

Then there are those who master something by getting deeper into the "why" of something. Such people may also look at others to understand what worked for them, but they never use that information without understanding it. They never seek a formula. This kind of person can become an entrepreneur.

Take for example a person I know, who lives in the Silicon Valley, doing well in his job in a famous company. I think Silicon Valley has some entrepreneurial rub-off effect on people, and so was the case with this acquaintance of mine. He was joining a group of entrepreneurs to start some tech firm. I cannot forget one particular conversation I had with him. He was sharing with me his entrepreneurial plans. On the top of his agenda was to fail. The funny thing was the way in which he said, "the idea is to fail early".

There is a prevalent thought in the world of entrepreneurship that early failures are blessings in disguise because they help you succeed later. Failure at an early stage helps you find the flaws in your assumptions, plans, approach, etc. It helps you course-correct sooner instead of failing at a larger scale later. The thing to understand here is, failure is not what makes someone successful. It is the ability to observe and learn from that failure. Many entrepreneurs don't learn from their failures, and continue to fail.

There is nothing glorious about failure. Failure is painful, and if you can succeed rather than fail, you'd rather succeed. In short, failure is not the goal. It's just that failure is inevitable. There is no formula, as straight forward as "early failure" = "success". Unfortunately, this classmate of mine had made failure the goal. He was running after a formula.

I find a lot of people posting on social media, doling out entrepreneurship formulas, like those 5-easy-steps-to-earning-a-billion-dollars. For example, start a company, do x number of meetings, get a few clients, build a large brand. They make it sound so simplistic. Interestingly, no seasoned entrepreneur, who has gone through the grind, built a large business will give out such formulas. They know just too well, there is no set path in entrepreneurship.

I also find many people lapping up these formulas eagerly. Just like we fall for those investment schemes that show us a simple calculation and how we can become a millionaire in a few years. I hear many newbie entrepreneurs say, how they are building the "next Google" or "next Apple". But here is the thing. If you are building the next Google and Apple, you are already, behind the curve. Way behind the curve. Someone thought of these companies 20 to 40 years ago. Yet many are trying to become like them today. If you really want to be Google and Apple, you have to foresee what will work 20 years from now. But a formula-driven mind simply fails to think this way. All they want is a tried-and-tested formula of success. A formula, that simply does not exist.

People who find themselves gravitating towards or looking for such formulas, might want to stay away from entrepreneurship. Alternatively, they could participate in a venture more in the role of a partner-employee, where they get equity and the tag of a partner, but function more like an employee in a senior position. There is absolutely nothing wrong with that. It takes all kinds of people to build a successful business, even the kind of people, who can do a good job once they have a formula to follow. It is just that, such people cannot be the lead entrepreneur in a start-up.

Let us just say that a real entrepreneur has a more discerning mind than others. He takes nothing at face value or as a formula. Not even if Steve Jobs hands it to him.

- **Hint #2: Got the guts?**

I was attending a conference of self-made millionaires. One of them said, "you don't need money and degree to be an entrepreneur; you need guts." Let us understand what this means. This thing called guts.

Man is a social being and we are all wired to be a part of the society. Being a part of society fulfils our need for connection. By belonging to a group, we draw a sense of identity; e.g. I belong to this culture, country, gang of friends in school, this group in college and I draw the meaning of "who I am" from it. The challenge comes when human beings are overwhelmed by the need to belong, and start subduing their original thoughts and views so as not to un-belong, or stand out too much.

A person with true entrepreneurial instincts is very much a social person, but without a strong need to belong to a group identity. This attitude is very important because entrepreneurship requires one to walk on a path with no guarantees. The ideas can be new and disruptive. There may be many nay-sayers. A person who draws his sense of identity from belonging and therefore approval of the group, will never be able to walk an uncharted territory.

Whether or not you get funding, you will get free advice by truckloads. These will be from well-meaning people such as peers, mentors, ex-bosses and experts. Sometimes it will also be from your family, spouse, parents and whoever else. These are people you don't want to displease. A true entrepreneur listens to everyone, but takes his own decisions, even if it deviates from popular opinion or expectations of any group or network.

He is a social being without an overwhelming need of validation or approval by the society, when it comes to decisions about his venture.

> *Guts of an entrepreneur is his conviction to follow his own mind,*
> *irrespective of who it displeases.*

- **Hint#3: Can you see what others miss?**

The top quality of a true entrepreneur is sensing opportunity. And that is simply a factor of being able to see a situation differently from others. Take any of the businesses that exist today; Uber, Dropbox, Facebook, and Apple. The opportunity for those businesses was open to everyone else in the whole wide-world. But the entrepreneurs who started them saw something, that others didn't.

> *Entrepreneurs see the dots, others don't and connect them in a way, others can't.*

There are many companies that could beat Apple at building computers. But Apple picked design as their niche and became the world's best at it; today they probably sell the world's most expensive laptops and phones. While everyone else defined the opportunity as electronics, Apple defined it as design. Steve Jobs saw something, others missed.

Anyone considering entrepreneurship should do a soul-search on how they have looked at things throughout their life. Have their view-points been a result of popular opinion, or what "experts" say; or, have they been a result of looking at something from very unique perspectives? A helpful exercise could be to look around in the environment, economy, politics and industry and try to think of how the next 5-10 years might look like in some areas of life. Reflect if your conclusions are based on what you have read in articles, blogs and talks; or are you able to draw some original conclusions of your own.

> *Originality in thinking is an undeniable quality of a true entrepreneur.*

III. A few more..

Apart from the qualities described above, I want to touch upon four other very important qualities of an entrepreneur.

1. Self-driven and disciplined

It is the ability to maintain the required pace of work without anyone else needing to follow-up. Essentially you are your own alarm clock. There is no boss coming after you to set deadlines, follow-up, question you why you did not do something. Most people are scared of this. They are afraid, that if they choose an entrepreneurial life, they may feel directionless. If a person cannot be self-driven, there is no way he can be an entrepreneur.

It is ironical. Many of us want to take up entrepreneurship because it gives us more control over our time. "I want to be my own boss", we say. However suddenly, when you have so much control over your time, things can get scary. Particularly, when you realize have paid the heavy price of quitting a job, or not taking a campus placement, to buy this time.

> *You can hold on to money. Unfortunately, you cannot hold on to time.*

In the initial phase of your start-up, you might be working alone, or with a few people. You don't have the regular "officey" things to do. Your days aren't filled with conference calls like other office-going people. What do you do on a day with no meetings? Do you while away the time? Watch all the whatsapp forwards in the world? Or do you spend that time atleast reading a book that will help you, benchmarking your competition, writing on social media to build your brand, or maybe working out to build fitness? This is also why I cannot talk about being self-driven without talking about discipline.

> *All our lives we have been systematically blinded to the distinction between discipline and obedience.*

We used to wake up on time because there was school and the fear of being punished for being late. We grow up, and we keep to schedule because of fear of the boss. Infact, many of my friends have categorically told me that they fear quitting their jobs, because they are not sure if they have the discipline to manage their time. No matter how much they dislike their jobs, it gives them a reason to wake up and do something constructive. It appears that, many of us, often, manage to do useful things with our time because of obedience to someone whether a teacher, boss or someone else.

Finding your own reason to wake-up and living a constructive day, even when there is no boss at your tail, is being disciplined. An entrepreneur needs to be that person.

2. Resilience

You can take hits and make a come-back every time. The importance of this quality cannot be over-emphasized.

> *Resilience simply means..*
> *what you do, on the next day, of a bad day.*

Do you go into depression? Do you lose focus and perspective? Do you start thinking of an exit route? Or, do you think, "okay yesterday was bad, but is there just one more thing for me to do today?" And go ahead doing that one more thing you know. That thing could be talking to just one more customer.

I write. It happens that many articles become trending back-to-back, and suddenly one does not do well. That article may be as good as the others; but it did not get as many views. Such things happen. Now what can I possibly do next? Simple. Write one more article. Resilience is simply.. that one more article.

Some of you reading this, might be quick to equate it to "never give up", in the sense of "never quit". That's not what I am saying. Let me also talk a little bit about quitting. I don't believe in "never quit". We have to quit. If you are an entrepreneur, you would have quit your job, isn't it? Quitting is a choice. We have to quit something or the other all the time. The question is:

> *Are you quitting as a matter of choice?*
> *Or are you quitting because you lack resilience?*

Sometimes you might quit, as a strategy, even if you have the resilience. But if you quit, when you shouldn't have, simply because you lacked resilience – now that is a problem.

3. Ability to get hands dirty

You can't build a business if you don't know the nuts and bolts of your core product. Infact ideally, you should know exactly how to do the job to some extent. A person who feels their job is only to sit in the corner office and never be on the shop floor, may become a CEO, but he can hardly succeed as an entrepreneur. An entrepreneur needs to be a grounded person that way. You need to have a hold on your products, employees and customers directly. For that, you need to roll up your sleeves as often as required.

You will read a lot of literature saying, "Don't be the best person in your team". This means you should hire people better than you, and not try to do everything yourself, etc. Let me put that kind of advice in perspective.

Firstly, the advice is correct.

- If you try to do everything by yourself – you will burn out
- If you are the best person at your job – you will find it difficult to trust others to do it aswell as you can

However, don't make the mistake of interpreting it as - you need not have in-depth understanding of the business, what the last-mile employee does and the customer feels. You may not do all the work yourself. But you can't afford to not have your ear to the ground. An entrepreneur should be prepared to roll up his sleeves whenever required.

Particularly people from senior roles in corporates, who are used to a large team doing things for them, might want to come prepared to make this mindset shift – should they choose to become entrepreneurs.

4. Metacognition

I have not seen this quality being talked about too often in the context of entrepreneurship. However, from personal observation, I think this is a very important quality of an exceptional entrepreneur. Metacognition simply means the ability to be aware of, and observe your own thinking.

For example, as an entrepreneur you need to take a decision, on whether to accept investment from a person who is imposing his own terms, which is not be suitable. Say you get a lot of advice to accept this investor, because he is well-known in the investment world. Accepting his investment may help attract other investors too. You have been told that if he walks out, it might discourage other investors. But you think that this investor is not right for your start-up. However, you get scared with all the advice and onboard that investor.

You give a logical reason to everyone that this investor brings a lot of strength to the table. More importantly, that is what you tell yourself. But, the real reason behind your decision was fear. The actual logical decision according to your assessment, was to reject the investor.

A person with metacognition will be fully aware of how these underlying emotions played in the mind and influenced the decision. He will not live under a false belief that he simply took a practical decision, instead of realizing the fact that it was a fear-driven decision. Metacognition is what helps the personal growth of an entrepreneur. This is what brings about that awareness, we discussed in Chapter I.

I know a young person, who is in the mid-career stage and wanted to join my business in a co-founder role. I have known him for a while, and in that duration, I have observed him to over-commit and under-deliver. He tries to do only as much is required, just when it is required – even though he has the potential to do more. Now here is the problem.

Sometimes, for things that are lower in our priority, it might actually be a good strategy to do just enough, just in time. However, that is a conscious strategy. The issue with this person is that he thinks he is doing exceptional quality of work; whereas the quality is average and effort could have been more. My apprehension of taking him onboard has been the complete lack of awareness of how he thinks and acts.

> *I can work with a person who makes mistakes.*
>
> *I cannot work with a person who makes mistakes, but is unable to be aware of it.*
>
> *Such a person will repeat mistakes. And that is not okay.*

Metacognition helps an entrepreneur observe this own thinking and become more mature over a period of time. He is able to improve his decision making as time passes. This is perhaps a rare quality, and has the potential to make someone an exceptional entrepreneur.

> *Everyone makes mistakes. Not everyone learns from mistakes.*

Metacognition, or being self-aware, is a way to learn from your mistakes. Entrepreneurs particularly need to learn quickly, or their survival may be threatened. I think being aware of your own thoughts also helps you bull-shit yourself less; give fewer excuses.

Entrepreneurs may or may not be brutally honest to the world. But they need to be brutally honest with their own selves. And that can happen only if you are aware of your thoughts and emotions; in other words, have metacognition.

IV. So is it your cup of tea?

The purpose of this chapter was to give clues to whether someone has the makings of an entrepreneur.

There are things called skills, and those can be learnt along the way. How to make a customer pitch, how to build products, how to manage finances, how to sell, how to ace social media, etc. are skills that can be learnt or hired. But the aspects we discussed in this chapter are seated deeper. It is about mental wiring. You cannot hire that externally. It has to come from within.

You cannot change your wiring overnight. Usually a change in mindset takes a lot of life experience, learning, introspection or some critical life incident. Hence, it may be a good idea to honestly evaluate oneself to see if these deep-seated qualities exist in you.

Presence of them may not guarantee success, but they ensure you can take a very good shot at entrepreneurship. Absence of them could mean, it is not really your cup of tea.

(Refer to the reflection guide on the next page, to reflect on whether you have what it takes)

Reflection guide for Chapter III

Finding if entrepreneurship is your cup of tea

1. Do you look for formulas in life? Do you find yourself attracted to people handing out tricks-and-tips?

2. On the contrary, how do you feel about people who make you 'figure things out yourself' – only give you guidance – not tell you the specific way of doing something? Do you like to figure things out yourself? (list a few instances in your life)

3. How have you taken important decisions of your life? Do friends, family or someone important to you professionally – influence your decisions? Have you been able to take decision which you were convinced about, but others were against? (list a few examples)

4. When decisions go wrong, do you own the decision, or blame someone (openly or mentally)?

5. How do you form your opinion about things? Do you consider different data points, views and form your own opinion? Or, do you get influenced by the opinion of few individuals? (list a few examples)

6. Are you able to sense opportunities better than your friends, peers? Are you the kind of person who finds a way to get things done, gather resources?

7. Have you done important things in your life on your own initiative? Or does someone need to chase you, be after you? (list few examples)

8. Are you the one who will roll-up his sleeves and get things done? Or do you enjoy a "senior" something tag, and order people around? Do you take accountability if things go wrong or blame your team?

9. Do you invest yourself in reflection, being aware of yourself? Or, do you get by your life unconsciously, mechanically?

10. Have you demonstrated resilience when things were tough, or you goofed up on something, in areas that mattered to you – professionally or personally? Could you continue pursuing a goal, making necessary course correction? (List few examples)

Chapter 4

FAMILY, DUTIES, INSTALLMENTS

I. Mother of all excuses to not become an entrepreneur

A vast majority of aspiring entrepreneurs will painfully recognize this one little sentence.

"I have a mouth to feed."

Infact, it is not one sentence, but a thousand questions hidden in those few words.

How much time will it take me to start earning as an entrepreneur? How do I pay the home and car EMI, my kid's school fees, and other bills till then? All my savings will be eroded; what if my venture fails? Is this a wise thing to do? We have to lower our standard of living; how will that feel like?

Etc.. etc.. etc..

These questions are definitely true of any mid-career stage professional who is contemplating quitting a job to become an entrepreneur. A just-out-of-college youngster who wishes to be an entrepreneur may not have as many financial responsibilities at that life-stage. However, they have their own challenges.

For example, there are cases where the family has pooled in all resources to educate this one child, and the expectation is that she or he will take up a job and take care of the siblings, parents, etc. Even if that is not the case, parents are worried about when you would "stand on your feet". Things get tougher when Bunty uncle's son, or Shyam

Sundar, the neighbor's kid, get a campus placement in an MNC, with good pay-package and foreign travel.

All factors put together, we can say that managing personal finances until the entrepreneurship venture starts earning profits, is a BIG question every entrepreneur has to answer. Ofcourse there is the ever-present risk that the venture may not take off at all. What is the way out for a normal person with no inheritance to count on? Let us see.

ENTREPRENEURS WHO WENT BACK TO THE CLOSET

II. Ways to feed the mouth and follow dreams, without freaking out

1. Mentally prepare yourself and your family

An entrepreneur must prepare not only himself, but also his family members, both mentally and emotionally. This is because:

> *Entrepreneurship is not just a career choice. It is a lifestyle choice.*

To prepare for this transition, an entrepreneur must map out different aspects of his life that are about to change. The exercise should involve family members whose lifestyle will be impacted. This is particularly important for the first few years before the venture really takes off.

Mapping involves discussing questions like:

- What are the living expenses?
- How much can we afford?
- What are we going to cut down?
- Will we not watch a movie every weekend?
- Will we need to cancel that holiday we have been saving for?

If this exercise is done over a period of time (atleast a few months), it will give more time to the family to adjust themselves to the new reality. People may take different amounts of time, and also react differently.

2. Simplify everything

Entrepreneurship is about choices.

Sometimes those choices are about saying YES. Experienced entrepreneurs will tell you that it is not always easy to know what to say yes to. They have to figure that out along the way. There is another type of choice one must make. This choice has to be made more frequently and with more clarity. It is the choice of saying NO. Saying no to anything that comes in the way of your goal, no matter how tempting it seems.

This begins with how an entrepreneur lives his or her daily life.

- Is maintaining 5 different credit cards important or does it take away your time and energy?
- Is maintaining 2 cars really required or can you manage with one and hire a taxi at other times?
- Do you want 2 laptops, 1 tab, 2 smartphones, 1 iphone, 1 smart watch or just one device will suffice?

> *You can spot a focused entrepreneur, from his ability to de-clutter and simplify his daily life.*

A lot of this decluttering involves family. I got convinced about the need to declutter a few years ago. This meant buying fewer things, using fewer services, having fewer possessions to maintain and manage. However, it took me about 1.5 years to get my entire family convinced. This is another conversation that aspiring entrepreneurs will need to have with their family.

> *De-cluttered living is a value.*
> *If you live with your family, then it has to become a family value.*

The way to do it – the way I convinced my family – was to help them see the value of it, to their personal lives. Let us face it. A family is a collective unit of individuals who have their own value systems, hopes and preferences of how they want to live life. For something to become a family value, everyone has to see what's-in-it-for-them.

Say you are the entrepreneur, and your wife has a regular job. You have lived your life a certain way till now. You are used to buying things at whim, things you may not end up using, but spending a lot of time and energy in maintaining, storing and repairing. You have decided to become an entrepreneur, which requires working even longer hours, think harder and have more financial discipline. You have evaluated that 50% of the things you have in your apartment are not used at all.

These include furniture, gadgets, clothes, and electronics, children's toys. The 50% of the things require you to buy a larger apartment. It takes a lot of time to clean and maintain. You have two cars and your favorite Harley, and you had to rent an additional parking lot. You even hired two people to help with the household work. Your new goal of leading a de-cluttered life now requires you to live with only half the possessions, and dispose the remaining. As a result of it you can live comfortably in a smaller home with lesser things to store and fewer support staff.

But, getting your family onboard (happily) can be more daunting than you can imagine. And ignoring this step of "family onboarding" in preparing for entrepreneurship can be riskier than you can imagine.

> *A supportive family can really give you strength in difficult times.*
>
> *A skeptical family can equally pull you down.*

Many people freak-out with the idea of having to sell-off things, especially when it coincides with one family member quitting a regular job and becoming an entrepreneur.

Family members may react as if, it is some ominous foreboding of things to come.

- So now we cannot even have a second TV?
- We cannot afford a second car, is it?
- Do we have to live in a smaller place?

None of these possessions may have anything to do with the happiness of any family member. Infact, often the family doesn't even notice the existence of these things until the day you decide to part with it. But people feel an immense sense of loss and deprivation if such a step has to be taken. The reason is simple. People associate amount of possessions with standard of living. Therefore, fewer possessions signal a drop in the standard of living, which feels scary.

REASON #59 FOR NOT LETTING GO

> *De-cluttering for entrepreneurship, also means learning to differentiate between,*
> *"standard of living" and "quality of life".*

The beauty of simple living is that it lets you focus on what is important. For example, should you be spending time thinking about your product idea or trying deal with issues of taking your cars for servicing and doing their insurance renewals? Simple living is choosing quality of life over standard of living.

> *Simple living is not about austerity. It is about priority.*

To convince your family members to adopt this kind of lifestyle you have to help them see and experience how it improves their personal lives. In the earlier example, maybe your wife is spending too much time in maintaining the house along with managing her career and the kids. Fewer things will create more time for her, to do things for herself – maybe that hobby of music or writing that book.

This is what helped me bring about the mindset change in my home, during my second entrepreneurial stint. Each of my family members were missing something that they wanted to do, but were stuck in the clutter. As soon as they experienced the joy of having more mental space, free time and energy, they completely bought into it.

One last word.

Clutter can be things. Clutter could be psychological, e.g. energy-sapping thoughts, emotions. There could be financial clutter, e.g. too spread out investments and loans. Clutter could be the social life you are leading, e.g. too many commitments. De-cluttering requires looking into each of them.

3. List the Money-Like-Resources (MLRs)

There is something that I heard Antony Robbins say during one of his talks, that I think all entrepreneurs should tattoo that on their arms if need be. He said,

> *It is not lack of resources,*
> *but your lack of resourcefulness that stops you.*

Why else is it that relatively well-off professionals give excuses like, if I had this, then I would do that. However, individuals who are actually deprived of resources: money, network, access – are able to build massive businesses. We traditionally we know these as the rags to riches stories. But these are really stories of revelation, because they reveal that building something is about the individual's imagination and not material resources.

So before beginning the entrepreneurial journey, it is important to make this shift in mental mode; that it is never the lack of money or other resources, but the lack of resourcefulness.

Also, you will realize that money is sometimes overrated. It is amazing how much you can get done without money, if you can really keep your eyes and ears open.

This is why it makes sense to maintain a list of what I call Money-Like-Resources (MLRs). MLRs are those which can either act as money and be used to get something done or can be used to generate money, without much effort.

Examples of MLRs are:

- A spare room you can put on Air BnB for an extra income
- A friend who clicks amazing pictures as hobby who can do a promotional photo shoot for you
- A relative who owns a house he can let you use as office address for registration until you expand enough to rent an office space
- A spare laptop, that you can pay as stipend to that bright college intern who did some pretty good work for you during summers
- Reward points on your credit card which you can use to buy office supplies on Amazon or air miles for your business travel
- Birthday or festive gifts that you may traditionally receive from members of family – ask them for

something that you can use for your business, e.g. instead of a phone that your parents or in-laws are planning to gift on your birthday – ask them to sponsor a small promotional event or an investor dinner that you may want to host

- Coupons, gift cards that you can use as payment in exchange of errands or corporate gifts
- Trial versions of software, D-I-Y tools

MONEY-LIKE RESOURCES (MLRS)

Let me share a personal example. I like to make communication visually appealing. Needless to say, that also has business benefits of getting attention from customers, potential employees, etc. At the initial stages of my start-up, hiring a marketing firm to make designer videos and communication, would cost me a bomb. So, I have used trial versions of tools like Canva, and select paid versions of many online tools, to create visually attractive communication myself.

If I had to pay a marketing firm, the equivalent of what I had created, would easily cost me atleast 1-2 lakh Rupees. I used MLRs of free versions, my own creativity and sweat capital to get the designs for no money. And it did generate marketing traction for me.

> *The list of MLRs can be as long as your creativity can make it.*

Apart from these, a key MLR that entrepreneurs use at early stage is equity. Equity can be used to pay salary, to raise money, get services, etc. However, the thing is – when the business is just about starting – there is no real value of it. Hence, how well you can convince others of the future value of your company will decide how best you can put equity to use. A word of caution. Not using equity well can lead to a lot of issues. Hence, if you are planning to get into entrepreneurship, this is one area you must seek to understand in your preparatory stage. I strongly recommend reading, Mike Moyer's, "Slicing Pie – Funding your company without funds", to understand how best you can leverage equity, when you don't have all the money you need. In my own entrepreneurial journey, while I have been resourceful in using MLRs, I realized equity is not something I understood well to begin with. I also realized that (a) it had a lot of potential value that can be used instead of cash; and (b) it needed to be used judiciously, else it could create more issues than benefits. Hence, my recommendation is that you spend some time developing your understanding of this, in your preparation for entrepreneurship.

Mastering Barter

The discussion on MLRs cannot be complete, without talking about barter.

At some level the global money system is rather unsophisticated. It is complicated for sure in all its variations and mechanism of operations. But it is unsophisticated. You need a service; you pay a price fixed for it in terms of money. You want better service you throw in more money; if you have less money you accept a lower quality of product and services. It is a system where the rich is powerful and can get anything. The poor is sidelined. The only thing that decides who is rich and who is poor is how much money you have.

Barter is different.

It seems simplistic on the surface, but it is a beautifully sophisticated system underneath. Barter is about understanding what the other person really wants and then trading it for something you want. The beauty of the barter system comes from the fact that different people want different things, and at different levels of desire. To barter successfully, you need to know:

- What someone really wants?
- How badly they want it?

In a barter system, you are rich not just by the amount of possessions you own but by your knack of understanding the other person.

Let's say you need the guidance of a seasoned entrepreneur. Now why would he spend his time and expertise on you? In your conversations you find out, the entrepreneur has a son preparing for his engineering entrance exams. Lo behold, you are one rock-star IITian. You offer to take a couple of sessions to help his son, and get a few sessions in return for business advice.

That is barter. But consider the same transaction using the money system. You would be paid some tuition fee for your entrance coaching classes. The advice from the entrepreneur, if charged, will be way more expensive. But the beauty of a barter system is everyone exchanges what they value. The entrepreneur values guidance to his son from an IIT-alum, and you value advice from a seasoned entrepreneur. It's at the same level. It's a win-win.

A word of warning.

Once an entrepreneur was trying to enter into a barter arrangement with me. She wanted me to write tons of articles for her. In exchange she offered me things like recommendation from her company and a testimonial video. This entrepreneur ran a small-to-medium, media company and has been in the business for a while. I was running a writing start-up which was new. However, she assumed that I did not have clients from whom I could get recommendations - and recommendations that I valued more, than hers. Also, she kept insisting on the immense effort that goes into making a video. I was not looking for an exotic video. My business was new. Its positioning would evolve with time. I was not sure what would the shelf life of a video be, at this stage. I was not looking at anything heavy-duty. In my eyes, these days, amazing videos can be made with just an iphone and free editing software – if you know the techniques and are adequately creative. Many You-tube influencers use just those tools make their videos. Additionally, this entrepreneur severely under-estimated the effort it took to write one good article. She wanted 'many-many' articles in exchange of 'one' video.

The outcome of these assumptions was predictable. The barter didn't go through. I could not see any value. So, here is the disclaimer we need to keep in mind. Barter is a fine art. You cannot use brute force like in the case of money. You have to really seek to understand the other person. The deal has to appear fair to both. No party must feel short-charged and manipulated. Infact, barter is a great lesson in "people skills".

Being able to identify and use MLR requires the sophisticated skill of observing what the other person wants, what you have, and exchanging it for something you need. A resourceful entrepreneur is one who can master the fine art of barter.

III. Don't find excuses, find a way

We began this chapter with that all-encompassing statement, "I have a mouth to feed". It sounds daunting and overwhelming enough, to send an aspiring entrepreneur running back to the closet. After all, what could be a nobler thing to do than to fend for one's family and children?

I am going to play the devil's advocate here. Not that, one should not provide for one's family. People who take up entrepreneurship have families too. Families they provide for.

> *But often people make their families an excuse,*
> *for not taking the risk to,*
> *do something they always wanted to.*

What is required is to look deep within, communicate with one's family and plan for the transition. There is nothing that cannot be achieved with good communication among those who love us. And, if you don't have the courage to do what you aspire to, atleast don't blame it on your family.

Finally, it is important to remember that entrepreneurship is a change for the family too. Often, they might not know or understand what is going on at work. However, they will be impacted by what is going on in your life. A supportive family is a boon for any entrepreneur – whether man or woman. It is important to involve them from the beginning, instead of making them a scapegoat. More often than not, our families will appreciate that.

Sometimes they may take time to come onboard - few months, maybe a few years. Don't feel frustrated that "no one understands me". You are in the thick of things. They are bystanders. They will never have a full view of the situation like you do. They may also come from a different value system; e.g. for your parents who had regular jobs all their lives, that was the most reasonable and respectable thing to do. Hence, they may not always understand your life choices.

Sometimes it is also about their worry and concern for you.

My father was an entrepreneur for a few decades of his career. We have seen a few ups and many downs, because of that. Our life experience of entrepreneurship had generally not been good. Hence, when I decided to take up entrepreneurship for the first time in 2013, my parents naturally freaked out. Here I was, having finally escaped the vagaries of my father's entrepreneurial life by studying from a top B-school and working for well-paying corporates. Yet, I wanted to throw it away for the same challenges we faced, during my growing up years. They feared for me, based on their life experience.

I was in-turn, upset with my mother, for being upset with me. My mom is the gutsiest person I know. She is my pillar of support. So, when I did not have her support, the first time I turned an entrepreneur, I felt angry. Even though I put up a brave face of, "I know what I am doing", I was scared just like any first-time entrepreneur. And here,

I did not get support from the person who mattered the most. Mom would not say anything. But the worry gnawing within was very visible on her face. "Why can't you be chill about this?" I would fight with her often. Even though she never explicitly told me the reason for her worry, until a few years later - I should have understood. Yet, I did not.

So here is what I am saying.

> *Even the most obvious emotions need to be explicitly discussed.*
> *Even among those, who are closest to us.*

The other word of caution, is to not buckle under these emotions. I returned to a corporate job after my first entrepreneurial stint. But it was my decision, which had nothing to do with how my mom felt abut it. I also returned for a second entrepreneurial stint. This time my mother was better prepared mentally, which worked well for me. But I would have taken another shot nevertheless. So, the second thing to remember is to stick to your convictions.

> *The worst thing we can do to our loved ones*
> *is to let them become the reason for giving up on our dreams*
> *and holding it against them, for the rest of our lives.*

I was clear that I would never let my family become the reason for not doing what I wanted to – and then be upset with them. The biggest entrepreneurial lesson this taught me was that every entrepreneur must build a combination of (a) being resolute about the path they want to follow; and (b) understanding the context of family members who react in a way, we don't want them to.

Even if they don't understand you, you should try and understand them. And the thing with family is, sooner or later, they eventually come around.

(Refer to the reflection quide on the next page to prepare your family and finances better.)

Reflection guide for Chapter IV

Reflection guide for preparing your family and finances better

1. Family

- Create a table such as below for each of your family members
- Write down the answers, it may not be as easy as it appears
- Think through the emotions, be specific. (E.g. 'Angry' is not the same as 'grudging')
- Revisit this document once in a while, in your journey, till your family is completely onboard
- Don't discount your children even if they are young. You may need to have some conversation with your 10-year-old kid aswell, if there aren't going to be grand birthday parties anymore

Family member #1	Parents, spouse, children (immediate family, especially dependents or those you are dependent on, others staying with you, e.g. joint family)
How will they be impacted by your decision to be an entrepreneur?	E.g. psychological impact (they will worry for you), lifestyle impact (can't travel or spend much), career impact (spouse has to stick to job)

How do they feel about it?	E.g. your spouse may feels resentful that you are putting the family's future to risk – or he/she may feel fearful – these are two different emotions
How do you feel about what they feel?	E.g. if your spouse feels resentful that you are putting the family's future to risk – you feel deeply sad that your spouse feels that way. Or, you may feel anger instead of sadness
How will you deal with it?	a. Dealing with family – e.g. what kind of conversations you need to have, give regular updates on progress, etc. b. Deal with yourself – be patient, understand their point of view, list what you can or cannot expect from them

1.   Finances

Spend some time creating an excel sheet of expenses and resources. It is advisable to build it over a period of time, as you might not remember everything at one go. If you have dependents or contribute to the family expenses (nuclear family, joint family, staying with spouse/parents/siblings), then it might be a good idea to involve some of them in this exercise. Even if you are just out of college and staying with/dependent on your parents, this exercise is important.

What are the absolute must-have expenses?	Food, rent, school fees (these are must-haves without which your survival is at risk), medical insurance (if your spouse does not have employer family insurance – you need to buy a private insurance policy)
What expenses can you do without?	These are all psychological (need for financial security) or social (what will neighbors/relatives think if we don't have this) – this is the tricky part – and an entrepreneur must have the guts to let go of things that are merely good-to-have.
How many months of survival money do you have?	It's your (SAVINGS divided by monthly MUST-HAVE EXPENSES) + some buffer for unforeseen expenses (assume no income/revenue for this time-period. If you do generate some money well and good. But your estimation must prepare you for the worst-case scenario – i.e. assuming no income)

How much initial money do you need for business?	This depends on the nature of your start-up. This is the amount needed for you to get your prototype up and running, generate initial revenue. (this is the "garage" stage of your business – you don't need to plan for grand office space, etc. Your expense is on the product development and delivery to initial customers). If you are including some angel investment in the calculation, it should be sure-shot money – not assumptions.
List all MLRs at your disposal	Spare laptops, reward points, customary gifts you receive from people, spare rooms that close friends/relatives can lend for office space, free tools/software, talent/skill (yourself/immediate family) you can put to use, all friends/colleagues/relatives you can reach out to for any help

Chapter 5

ABOUT KEEPING A SIDE JOB

I. Maintaining cash-flow while business is getting built

Professionals quitting a full-time job to try entrepreneurship, often try keeping a side job - partly for supplementary income and partly due to fear of completely letting go of a career they have taken so many years to build. They try to keep a "fall-back" option. Letting go completely is not easy, especially when the road in front of you is fuzzy and you are very likely to make a brief acquaintance with failure. However, it is this fear of letting go, that causes errors in judgement while choose a side job.

Depending on the nature of your business venture and number of partners, cash flow may take time to build. The time could vary from a few months to few years. Entrepreneurs start off with a small pool of money that will pay their bills for some time. Usually the time advised is 12-18 months. But things in an entrepreneurial journey are always variable. Getting income from your business may take longer. Funding is not assured. Hence, you cannot always count on getting any basic salary to pay your bills.

In addition to that, is the psychological factor. When I was in my first entrepreneurial stint, there were two months when I made very little money. To put things in perspective, I had quit my job to try entrepreneurship without any real financial preparation. (Remember I said in Chapter I, that this was my phase of I-did-know-that-I-did-not-know. And one of those things I-did-not-know was that you should keep a buffer of 12-18 months before you take the plunge).

Hence, these two months of meagre revenue really put me in a state of panic. Basically, what I am saying is, that the psychological factor – the fear, can be terrifying. I can tell you that from first-hand experience. But I don't want you to get scared (remember, I came back to try entrepreneurship again). I just want you to prepare better.

For a person who had a job earlier, to not have any earning for 12 to 18 months can be mentally unnerving. A college pass-out, who gave up campus placements, also has his moments of nervousness. His friends now have jobs. They are enjoying their first salary; partying, buying a new car, shopping. All this while, he is still dependent on his parents for expenses. Mostly likely the parents are worried that their child has not 'settled down', while everyone else has.

Therefore, identifying a few alternative sources of income might not be a bad idea. It could keep the cash coming in, even if a trickle here or a dribble there. It takes care of your expenses and keeps up your morale. However, here is the caveat that every entrepreneur must remember:

> *Those alternative sources of income are just that.*
> *Alternatives.*

They should never take focus away from the core business you left a job to establish.

II. Kind of side job you should look for

I call it the ADHD criteria (no, not attention deficit – but it will be easier to remember this way), a set of 4 principles that any entrepreneur can apply while selecting a side job.

Auto-pilot **D**iscreet **H**armonious **D**issolvable

ADHD CRITERIA TO CHOOSE A SIDE JOB

AUTO-PILOT	CAN BE DONE WITHOUT STRAIN
DISCREET	NOTHING TOO PROMINENT
HARMONIOUS	NO CONFLICT WITH BUSINESS OR PARTNERS
DISSOLVABLE	LOW EXIT BARRIER

Following is what it means:

Side-job should be on Auto-pilot (A of ADHD criteria)

The side-job should not require too much effort from you, either in terms of time or mental bandwidth. The following is what I mean by "auto-pilot":

- **It should be a skill or source of income that is readily encashable**

E.g. you find that you can make some money on the side by becoming a blogger. But you are not such a great writer, and the skill itself needs to be developed first, which requires time and mental bandwidth. It is a bad idea.

On the contrary say you are good at math. If you give math tuitions for an hour at home or teach at the neighboring coaching classes, that is better. You already know the job and you can do it on an auto-pilot mode.

Similarly, say you own a piece of land, which you decide to put to use as an alternative source of income. But you are thinking of first constructing two floors and then renting it out as a paying guest facility. Even if you have the money to build the two floors, it is a bad idea. It will take away time and focus from what you have started out to do.

Instead, it is a better idea to give it to a property builder on lease. Or, if you have a cousin or friend who is capable of getting it done, pay him to manage it on your behalf.

A focused entrepreneur will think:

This arrangement with my cousin will mean spending some money (because the cousin will take his share), but it saves me 15 hours in a week. It is a good deal.

A naïve entrepreneur will think:

I have stopped earning a salary, so every penny counts. I must do this myself and not share the money with my cousin. This entrepreneur will spend 15 hours a week in setting up a side income – while having given up a much larger income to get those 15 hours! I hope you see the point.

Often, we don't realize that,

> *TIME is a more important resource than MONEY.*

Many people make a mistake here, because they don't know what to do with their time. You cannot be an entrepreneur if you don't realize the power of time and how to put it to use.

- **It should be task-based, with clear deliverables**

For a job to be on auto-pilot, it needs to have a defined set of tasks and goals, with a definite start and end time. For example,

Coach 5 people for 1 hour each, every Friday for 3 months

V/s

Consulting assignment of helping the sales team improve team work over the next 3 months, including needs analysis, finding solution, planning and delivering sessions

The second type of assignment is going to get you killed. The problem with this kind of consulting assignments are:

- They roll over beyond scheduled time, in form of calls, emails
- The project duration tends to get extended
- Lot of coordination may be required for which time cannot be estimated
- It takes a lot more mental space

If you have quit your regular job at a middle management or senior level, you might be particularly tempted to take these up. Often people are consciously or unconsciously keeping a back-up option. They are trying to stay relevant, keep their network alive and avoid "rusting". If the business fails, they have something to fall back on. These assignments also tend to make you feel significant and valued by the industry (i.e. someone still cares for your advice) – and remind you of the "good old days".

But if that was the most important thing for you, why did you quit it for entrepreneurship? Why do you want to spend your time earning a fraction of your earlier income, in doing part-time what you had a full-time job for? Should you not rather keep your full-time job?

They say, you cannot fly until you let your feet get off the ground. You also cannot swim if you insist on staying on the shore. If you pick up assignments that consume most of your energy and time, in order to keep a back-up option, that very act might ensure that your failure.

> *Entrepreneurs must never forget that entrepreneurship is their full-time job.*

Any side job should be taken keeping that in mind. If you have to choose between a challenging consulting assignment versus a smaller task with clear tasks deliverables, accept the latter; even if it appears less important or pays lesser.

Side job should be Discreet (First D of ADHD)

Your side job needs to be low-profile. You should never be seen doing your side job (e.g. you posting on social media about something to do with your side job). You should only be visible for your main entrepreneurial venture. If you are seen doing too many things, your audience (customers, investors, evangelists), will be confused with what to associate you with. In short, your personal brand (which is very important, reference our discussion in Chapter I), will go for a toss.

To keep your job discreet, the following is recommended:

- **Don't be seen publicly for anything except your core business**

We live in the age of social media, and rely heavily on it for promotion of our business. Apart from social media campaigns under the business name (e.g. the LinkedIn company page), an entrepreneur invariably uses his personal social media network to promote his business. Infact, personal promotion is more dominant during the initial days of a start-up; when the start-up itself is not so recognized. Which is why, it is so important to remember – that you should never promote or solicit work or sales on the public domain, when it comes to your side job. At the cost of repeating myself, I will say it again. Be seen only for your main entrepreneurial venture.

People should know you as the founder or co-founder of that one business you are promoting at this point in time, and not any other side-work you might be doing. It is good to remind oneself that an alternative source of income has to be "on the side"; never in the forefront, never known too publicly.

- **Don't reach out to the same network for many different things.**

Say you have a set of close-knit friends in the professional arena. You are trying to set up a business and also building some alternative sources of income (like putting your property on lease). Most common approach is to reach out to that same set of people because you are comfortable with them. That might not be the best idea.

You must reserve your most dependable contacts for help in the most important areas of your core business.

Side job should be Harmonious (H of ADHD)

The alternative source of income must never interfere with any aspect of the core business. It should allow you to be available completely and whenever required for your main business. Balancing the core business and a side job requires some bit of planning. However, you must never have to compromise on any aspect of the core business for a side job. Some of the following must be considered to ensure that the side job is harmonious to the core business:

- **Harmony of schedule**

The number of hours, timing and travel requirement of the side job must align with the core business schedule. Does your role in the core business require you to work more in the morning or late night? The side job timing should complement that. Does your core business or side business require you to travel? If it will keep you away from being present for your core job, a travel related side job must be avoided. During my second entrepreneurial stint, I write professionally. I have had to consciously think through, the nature of contract I sign with companies. Flexibility of schedule and predictability of work are important criteria for me. Also, I insist on having minimal number of stakeholders to deal with.

- **Harmony of business interest**

Say, you have started a venture with a few partners in an industry. You are a technology expert or content expert. Another company reaches out to you for a consulting assignment to build similar (not same) tools or content - as what your venture is planning. No matter how tempting and lucrative it sounds, and how easy it will be for you to deliver this project, it is probably best avoided.

Small start-ups may not get you to sign a "conflict of interest" like large corporations. Many things work on verbal understanding. But being mindful of conflicts of interest is just as important in a start-up. Infact, I will say that it is of paramount importance, because that is the time trust gets built among partners. If something runs the risk of a conflict of interest or raises doubts in the minds of your partners, it is best avoided. Also, your actions set the tone of business ethics among partners and initial set of employees.

> *To put it simply, you should avoid doing anything, for a side-income, that you will not want your partners to do.*

- **Harmony in partnership relations**

No side job should be hidden from the partners. Partnerships are very delicate relationships, and trust takes time to develop. Keeping a side job, without the other partners' knowledge might lead them to trust you less, feel cheated or even create a perception that you are not contributing much to the business. All of those could be fatal for the business, and not worth whatever money you earn from the conflicting side assignment.

Other partners might be on the same boat as you, and therefore an open discussion on what all partners collectively think about side jobs might be useful. Among partners, there can be:

- Full disclosure of any existing side jobs
- Agreement on ground rules on side jobs – hours, nature of job, for how long, etc.
- Agreement on outcomes each must deliver despite any side job
- Agreement on setting boundaries - that once disclosure is made, and as long as all deliverables are met, a side job should not be any partner's concern

Side job should be Dissolvable (Last D of ADHD)

Side job is meant to be temporary, until the start-up is off the ground, funding is in or some such logical milestone. Any side job should have a low exit barrier.

You should be able to stop doing it without creating difficulties for those who have employed you, at the notice of a few weeks, if required. It should be easy to do a knowledge transfer quickly. You need to be firm, and insist on a backup resource, you can train from the beginning, if the nature of assignment be such. Ofcourse, you can just stop the side work giving no notice, but that will spoil the goodwill with the person who gave you the side job. You represent your business. If the business takes off, you don't want anyone to feel you "dumped" them. It is not the right thing to do. Choose a side job with fewer stakes, which is easier to dissolve. And set clear expectations on your priorities, right at the beginning.

In conclusion, a side job might be a necessary evil. But it is important to remember that it is just to support the main venture – the start-up for which you took all the risk. Focus is very important. So is time. Don't choose a side job which pays you some money but takes away a lot more focus and time. Let a side job remain on the side.

Remember the principle of A-D-H-D.

(Refer to the reflection guide on the next page to assess if the side-job is right for you.)

Reflection guide Chapter V

Assessing if a side-job is suitable for you

I. Can it work on Auto-Pilot?

1. Are you already proficient in the skills required to do your side-job (i.e. you can deliver it without a struggle)?
2. Are the timing and deliverables of your side-job, well-defined and fixed?

II. Is it Discreet?

3. Does the side-job require you to be visible on social media?
4. Does this side-job require you to use your close professional connections?

III. Is it Harmonious?

5. Does the work-timing of your side-job conflict with your start-up's work?
6. Is the nature of side-job in any kind of conflict of interest with your start-up?
7. Are your partners okay with your side-job? Have you been transparent with them?

IV. Is it Dissolvable?

8. Can you exit your side-job on a very short notice?
9. Can you exit your side-job without hassle or heart-burn?

Chapter 6

HOW BIG A BUSINESS SHOULD YOU ASPIRE TO BUILD?

I. Scale is not the only measure of value

There is this amazing little burger place in Bangalore, India. At its full capacity, it can seat upto 70-80 guests. You can call it a small business. I have never tasted burgers so delicious anywhere in my life. I have had gourmet burgers in several places in the US, but this eatery in Bangalore will have you drooling. Not to mention their pancakes, sandwiches, eggs of all kinds. Infact, during my various trips to this restaurant, I have come to conclude that anything you order here, tastes out of the world. On weekends, you will have to wait for a table. Should they want to scale, nothing will come in their way of finding investors or being assured of customers queuing up at their door. Yet they operate at just two locations in the same city.

There is a private school in the west of India, that I visited. It is a one of its kind institution; a benchmark among schools. They have exceptional to approach to children and learning. Who's-who of education globally, have visited and lauded the school. The annual intake is about 400-500 learners as I was given to understand. They get 5 times the number of applications every year. If the school today wants to scale up several times, they will have no dearth of investors, educationists and learners. Yet the school leader is very clear that they would choose to be a center for excellence and thought leaders rather, than dilute the learning culture by burdening themselves with scale. True to their mission, they are doing phenomenal work in sharing best practices and research with a large number of other educationists, who then go back to their own schools and implement the learnings. This school has chosen to stay small in size, but has high impact on the education community.

On the other hand, there are likes of McDonalds which are behemoths in their area. There are the franchisee educational institutions that boast of opening scores of new branches every academic session.

I am making this contrast so that all aspiring entrepreneurs understand one thing about the scale of business. Scale is not the only measure of the value a business adds to the society.

> *Valuation and value are not the same things.*

II. All businesses are not same

All businesses do not lend themselves to scale in the same manner, due to differences in nature of product and services, operating model, service delivery – and even mission.

> *There is no rulebook that says until your business is worth a million it is not a worthy business.*

If you create something of value for customers, create an organization where employees are happy, make decent profits, and are able to sustain the business amidst market changes - it is a good business. Even if it is small. Let no one tell you otherwise. You can build a business that brings millions in revenues. You can also build a business to replace your corporate salary.

> *In the matter of, how big a business you should build, each one to his own.*

Say you were earning 30 lakhs annually in your full-time job, which you quit to become an entrepreneur. You built a business that lets you earn profits of the same amount or a little more – is that a bad thing? Earlier, you earned that money being a cog in a large wheel. Now you earn the same money creating a new business, employing ten people, serving one thousand customers – expanding your capability across multiple domains. Is it bad or is it better? Are you going to feel happier about yourself? Are you not making a bigger contribution to the society, as compared to when you were in your regular job?

> *Objective of becoming an entrepreneur, is not limited to earning more money.*
>
> *It can also be earning the same money, while making a bigger contribution.*

If you can build another Google, Uber and Apple – good for you. But if you want to build a robust business serving just the local community, you should not feel any less proud. There are many capable professionals who take a conscious call to build a niche business of limited scale. The reason could be the nature of business itself, or what they want to achieve personally though the business.

> *The world may have opinions about the size of your ambitions.*
>
> *But your decision should be rooted in what you want.*
>
> *Not what the world thinks, you should want.*

How Big a Business Should you Aspire to Build?

Remember the thing we discussed about a real entrepreneur following his own guts rather than popular opinion (Chapter III, "Is it your cup of tea"). The scale you want your business to achieve is also about following your own gut and taking your own decision.

> *It is your life, your dreams and your call.*

Ideally, I should not be talking about "scale" at this stage of the book. It's something for Part II of the book. The reason I am touching upon this topic, is that you get asked the "scale" question even before you have found validation for the business. "How will you scale the business", people start asking – even while you are still validating the idea. So, it helps to be clear about the fundamentals of scale. At this stage, you don't need to worry about how to scale. At this stage, simple know, that any scale you decide on, is fine.

Another invisible social pressure on entrepreneurs is the popular diktat:

Successful business = large scale

But that is not the truth, no matter how much of popular literature is dedicated to it. Entrepreneurs forget that the first and most fundamental question about their business is: "what is the core value the business is adding to a customer's life?"

After this question has been answered, you need to figure out what is the best way of delivering that value. Only after that - do you start thinking about scale. And the most important thing to understand about scale is that, scale is NOT how much revenue this business can generate.

> *Scale is how many more customers can be served without compromising on the intended core value of the business.*

I say this because, in the enthusiasm to scale, if entrepreneurs fail to maintain the core value proposition, that very scale will take the business down. For example, the customers loved the personalized service when you started the business. As you scaled, you started standardizing everything – removing the very things customers liked about you. That kind of scale is counter-productive.

All of this is not to say, you should not scale. If you can, please do. What I am saying is that the most important metric is the value you are adding. Keeping that value intact, if your business can scale – great. If not, it is perfectly okay to run a small business.

III. Investor mandate v/s Founder mandate

Scale is also often driven by investor interests. By the very virtue of their role, an investor's primary interest is to get maximum returns on their investment in the shortest possible time. So, entrepreneurs grapple with the pressure of not just scale, but also speed of scaling. We have seen disastrous cases of start-ups which have scaled too fast too soon. Businesses scale with unsustainable offerings, false promises, weak service infrastructure and unprepared teams - finally leaving all stakeholders in a lurch. A complete lose-lose.

Investors bear the first loyalty to their investment. A founder must owe his loyalty to the business. Mostly, those two paths coincide. Sometimes, they don't. The moot point in all of this is, before you have started with your business, your thought should be about what do you care for enough, to start a business in that area. How you will scale needs to come much later.

> *Founders must stand by the core intent the business was built for,*
> *even when the investors won't.*

The business world is reaching a nauseous level of obsession for:

- Let us build an "Uber-of-something"
- Let us gamify it
- Let us appify it

All of these are largely driven from the notion that any aggregation, gamification and app are easily scalable and sellable. They might also get funding much easier. If what you are building, lends itself naturally to any of these, great. If not, for God's sake do not feel compelled to limit your imagination to what everyone else is doing.

Human beings are not pigeons or monkeys; they can learn using far advanced methods than just collecting reward points and competing with others. Gamification is popular, but it represents the lowest form of learning (do work-get rewarded-compare yourself). Similarly, apps cannot replace direct human interaction. I have nothing against gamification or apps; I use them as a customer. But I am bringing this up to make just one point. Just because something is popular, doesn't mean you should feel compelled to do it. This is the part where we said a real entrepreneur uses his own mind.

So, on the question of scale; remember it is okay if you want to build a business that serves a hundred customers, or one that serves a hundred million – as long as you make sure your service is worth the customer's time, money and attention. And it has to be your own decision.

> *Don't choose a business based on "how much I can expand it".*
>
> *Choose a business based on "how much I care for it".*

Another false metric of scale is, number of employees. Google search the list of "Small Giants" by Forbes (list of best small companies). You will find enough and more examples of million-dollar companies built with very few employees. So please, don't fall into that trap either. Just because you are now measuring scale, by number of people you employ, instead of revenue – does not make scale-for-the-sake-of-scale more noble or less problematic.

It takes all kinds of entrepreneurs to make the business world. A dark horse has as much of a place, as a unicorn. The world is after unicorns these days. If you are building a business, focusing on building the roots, your growth may not be visible to the world anytime soon. You are likely to be ignored. But just like a dark horse, you will establish your worth, when the time comes.

Build your business the way you want to. That is the only thing that matters.

Chapter 7

ARE YOU READY TO TAKE THE PLUNGE?

I. The decision point

There is a king in Indian Mythology called Trishanku. He wanted to go to heaven while still alive. This was against the natural laws and therefore the Gods wouldn't allow it. Trishanku is remembered till today because his desire to go to Heaven alive, left him hanging midway between the living world and the heavens. He is a metaphor for being in a state of 'neither here nor there'.

Many aspiring entrepreneurs wait for the "right moment" to switch from a regular job to entrepreneurship. They are Trishankus halfway between their regular job and the new venture.

Sad part is some of them, stay that way, for too long.

"When is the right time to take the plunge?" This is a question that all aspiring entrepreneurs think about. Some are able to take a decision based on some criteria of their own. Some rely on advice from others. Few are never able to decide.

"Am I ready to take the plunge", is not a single question. It is a composite of readiness across 3 dimensions.

- Have I saved enough? (Financial Readiness)
- What is the state of readiness of my new venture? (Business Readiness)
- Am I prepared mentally? (Psychological Readiness)

II. Readiness to start

Financial Readiness

It is commonly advised that you should have 12-18 months of survival money saved at the time of leaving. If you have school going kids, you may want to keep aside school expenses for a little longer, maybe 2 academic years.

Financial readiness consists of 3 categories.

- **Finance category #1: Basic living expenses**
  - Rent
  - Food
  - Amenities
  - Support staff
  - Planned travel
  - Known travel budget
  - Small entertainment budget
- **Finance category #2: Unforeseen emergencies and medical requirements**
  - Insurance cover for health and life

Many working professionals rely on insurance policies provided by the employer. In countries like India, group insurance has significant benefits like coverage of pre-existing diseases and senior parents. If you have an inkling that you might want to become an entrepreneur in future, some foresight in this area will be helpful. Evaluate individual insurance policies and how many years you need to have them for, to cover pre-existing diseases and make an investment in it. E.g. take an individual medical insurance over and above your office insurance 2-3 years before you want to become an entrepreneur – so that by the time you leave, it has reached the "covers pre-existing diseases" stage.

- A kitty to tap in for any unforeseen emergencies

This kitty may have some money, and assets you will be able to encash quickly if needed. Quickly is the key word. A property takes time to liquidate. You may have jewelry or some shares, etc., which you can sell fast. This is only worst-case scenario. You may not get there at all. You cannot prepare for all exigencies. But it is practical to atleast have one line of defense in case you need.

- **Finance category #3: Business expenses**
  - Cost of incorporation
  - Legal paperwork, etc.
  - Website
  - Initial branding and promotion
  - Any customer research
  - Business travel
  - Cost of production and delivery (for initial set of customers)

The amount may vary depending on whether you have business partners, type of incorporation, angel funding, etc. A common advice is to build a prototype while you are working. I know of many professionals who use their spare time to build a business on the side. Doing that, is sometimes possible. Sometimes it is not. There is no rulebook. Someone may decide that they want to give their complete attention to entrepreneurship. In that case, you should have a small fund to build a prototype and get a few customers to validate your solution. At this stage, you don't need a fancy office. This is what they call the "garage stage".

A friend of mine started with her art business from home. She did not even have a website. She focused on the core product which became popular through word of mouth and Facebook. She will get a website and all the jing-bang in due time. But the sensible thing to do is to focus on building your core product or service. You may be in a business which needs a good website to begin with - but an office or full-time employees may not be required. Important question to ask oneself is: "What do I really need at this stage to start the business, and what should come later?"

For the first website of my second start-up, I did not want to spend much. Initially, I tried hiring some freelancers. When that did not work, I took some Word press DIY template and made a fairly decent website. It was good enough for me to get customers for the first leg of my start-up. The next version of the website will need significant investment and hiring actual pros. But that is after the business has completed the validation stage of finding paying customers.

The same principle applies to living expenses too. You have to decide what is really necessary and what is not. Unfortunately, if you happen to have done well in your corporate career and built a standard of living around it – foreign holidays, frequent dining out, expensive gadgets, unnecessary furniture, clothes, accessories – you run the risk of your own lifestyle coming in the way of your aspirations.

Stories of all people who made a mark in the world, whether as entrepreneurs or other professions, have one thing in common:

They risked giving up good, for great.

From Elon Musk to Mark Zuckerberg to Bill Gates – they all had the privilege to go to Ivy League colleges that could have given them a high paying job with a very comfortable lifestyle. Yet, they all chose to live relatively ordinary lives at the beginning of their career to achieve something great. If they had bothered about club memberships and cars at that stage in their life, they would have had good lives – but not great. If you are hung up on the frills of life, you might aswell continue in your current job. But if you are taking a conscious decision to create something through entrepreneurship, you might have to give up some of the extravagance.

Basic lifestyle does not mean you start skipping meals. It means a lifestyle that is lean, simple and effective – i.e. it allows you the time, energy, space and money you need to invest in your entrepreneurship. Simplifying lifestyle does not only mean reducing; it also means replacing.

- Replacing unhealthy food habits with healthy ones, because you cannot afford to fall ill. That will cost money and time away from work

- Replacing ways, the family bonds together. People just take for granted that you have to work 24/7, so family needs to be neglected. That is not true. You can plan and find ways for the family to connect, through ways that is less expensive but more meaningful. Maybe twice a week family meal or a family movie on television or some common activity.

You won't have much time, but set aside something small – and make it sacrosanct. You would want your family around you to celebrate when you have "made it". That may not happen automatically. You have to deliberate work on that aspect too.

> *Entrepreneurship can be a long haul.*
> *Don't keep relationships on the back burner*
> *forever.*

Make a transition that is manageable and sustainable, not just for you - but your family. Don't go from movies every weekend, to none at all. Maybe keep provision for one in a month, or whatever is sustainable.

Try answering the following questions:

- How often are you eating out and shopping? How much is that reducing from your pocket? How much is it adding to your health, enjoyment and family bonding? Is there another way to fulfil the needs of good food, family bonding and entertainment?

- How many house-helps do you need? Are you utilizing them completely? Is your lifestyle too complicated? Is there too much wastage? Do you have just too much furniture and things to maintain?

- How many installments do you have? This is a significant roadblock for many aspiring entrepreneurs. They weave their life around debt. Modern day economics sometimes leads us to believe in some distorted notions of financial well-being. People pay significant installments on a home, with the hope of creating an asset. Unfortunately, till you have paid off the very last installment, the bank is the owner of the house, not you. People also buy depreciating items such as cars and electronics on finance.

If you want to become an entrepreneur you have to seriously consider simplifying all the installments you might be paying. You may even have to take a few tough calls.

- Do you really need that luxury sedan you are paying the installment for, or will a hatchback transport you just the same? (if keeping up appearances in front of neighbors and colleagues feels too important, you may not be the entrepreneur type)
- Do you want that 4-bedroom flat or a 3-bedroom will do just fine?
- Do you want all those electronic devices? Do you even use 20% of the functionality?

I am not going make any judgement on whether or not you should aspire for these. You have to take a judgement call on what you want more. Preparation for entrepreneurship should begin atleast one year before you decide to take the plunge. The year should be spent in simplifying one's life and lifestyle. It takes time, and involvement of the family. Having done the above, one should be reasonably prepared financially to take the plunge. The other aspect for aspiring entrepreneurs to think about is business readiness.

Business Readiness

It includes questions like:

- I still haven't decided on an idea, should I wait till I am sure?
- I have an idea; maybe I should get some validation and then leave my job
- Maybe I should start the business operations while on job and then leave

Aspiring entrepreneurs can be found at various points of readiness. But which is the correct state to be in?

In my first entrepreneurial stint, I was ready with a website at the time of taking the plunge. In my second stint, I only had a couple of ideas, and took a few months after quitting my job to develop the ideas, select the one I wanted to work on first, and then prepare for the launch, etc. The thing to consider is the nature of your current job.

- How time-consuming is it?
- How much travel is required?
- How mentally exhausting is it?
- Are you in a challenging project right now, which requires complete involvement?

A lot is going to depend on how much time and energy you have to start building your new business, while at your current job. I will go back to the popular advice I mentioned earlier – about building the product prototype while you are at a job. However, once again I will say that – it cannot be a rule. Some people have jobs that require you to work long hours, travelling and being on-calls constantly. Such people will find it difficult to build a business on the side. Either, you will need to take up a low-profile job for a while – or quit the job and then attempt entrepreneurship.

There is a concept called **hidden hours.**

Successful people have a few hours tucked away every day or week where they work on things that will help them in the long run. They do not publicize these. These are hours when others might be in pursuit of entertainment – watching TV, playing video games, going to the mall. But some people use it for things like learning a new skill, building business plans, networking, reading and writing.

> *How prepared you are to take the plunge also depends on*
>
> *whether you had hidden hours tucked away working to prepare yourself*
>
> *while others were watching Game of Thrones.*

Building a venture takes a lot of research to begin with. You have to start familiarizing yourself about various aspects of entrepreneurship; success stories, failure stories, industries, technologies, how a business is run, finances, types of incorporation, paperwork, etc. This is just to get you warmed up. You won't learn everything by reading. You will also not avoid all mistakes just because you read about them. Not everything will make sense until you actually experience it. Still reading helps.

While considering business readiness, you must also factor in, your readiness in having developed a broad understanding of entrepreneurship. It is a good practice to have spent a few months reading extensively before taking the plunge. Irrespective of the nature of your current job at least some amount of reading can be accommodated; maybe while commuting to work, on flights, during breaks – a 10-minute here, a 10-minute there. This part of the preparation is doable in almost any kind of job. If you can't make time for this, it is probably a sign that you will not be able to manage your time well as an entrepreneur either.

The next question is - should you have a business idea ready, before taking the plunge?

It is nice if you do. Even if you have not finalized it, atleast some clarity in what area you might want to start a business in, helps. In case you find yourself swinging across opening an ice-cream lounge on one end and a travel company on the other – maybe you should take some more time to get clarity. But if you know, it is going to be an eatery – but need to finalize what type, you may choose to get that clarity after leaving your job (provided you have financial and psychological readiness).

Finalizing an idea needs mental focus. If you have lot of responsibilities at work, it might be difficult to focus.

If you are heading an important project or juggling a lot of responsibilities, you may not have the focus required to take a decision on a business idea. In such circumstances, unless it is possible for you to opt for a low-key project at work, you may choose to finish your current job, and take time off to think. I know of a senior technology leader who cut himself off everything, including social media to focus on thinking of his product. So, there are no rules about it. Do what is required to give yourself the time you need.

The next question is if you should start with the business operations while you are still working.

This one is slightly tricky and grey. You have to consider if you are in any real conflict of interest with your current job. If that is ruled out, you still have to do the work under the radar. There could be troublesome grapevine and assumptions should your colleagues or manager get to know of it. Even if you are not in any real conflict of interest, your current employer will never be happy knowing you have a business venture on the side. They will also start speculating about your impending resignation. A question you must ask yourself is whether you can really do justice to both jobs at the same time.

One of the many reasons for business partnerships to fail is, few partners continue in their day job when it is time to establish the business. Is that what you want?

I personally feel you cannot do much keeping your feet across two boats. A start-up takes every ounce of energy, imagination and resourcefulness that founders can put it.

> *Two-timing your start-up, may not be the best idea.*

I know of a person who has started this software company with partners while still in the current job. He has to go lengths to keep it under wraps, including using an abbreviated form of his actual name in the official email id of his new company. It can get tiring.

So, the final question is, what are you afraid of?

PSYCHOLOGICAL READINESS

In August 2017, I wrote this post on LinkedIn. I did not expect anything much from it at the time of posting it. But it got more than 138,000 views. I was taken aback at how many people instantly resonated with it. The post was a comparison between being in a regular job versus entrepreneurship. I actually expected entrepreneurs to maybe like it, and job-goers to not like it. But the comments were mostly from those on regular jobs, saying how accurately it described their situation. The post in verbatim was this:

I know why people continue in jobs they sometimes don't even like much.

Being on a job is like being on a train that will move, and you just need to be on it - to move with it.

You may choose to run, walk or just sit on the train and you will still feel - life is moving.

You can't run ahead of the train, nor stay behind it.

You maybe be on the first-class compartment. Or, in one with stinky toilets.

But the train, and you with it, will move. That is guaranteed.

Working on your own, is like going to the engine cabin and putting the coal in, every single day for the train to move.

Watching if the train is headed in the right direction, and on track.

You are neither ahead nor behind the train.

You, become the train.

The worst fear of quitting one's job is not loans, bills, and savings.

The worst fear of quitting one's job, is whether you will have the energy every single day to go to the engine cabin to put the coal in.

> *To keep the fire burning.*
>
> *On some days, I dream of being on the train that moves on its own.*
>
> *It will be nice to not face the furnace.*
>
> *Alas, it may take me to a destination far away from mine. The engine, coal and soot are waiting for me on another one.*

This I think sums up the essence of psychological readiness. You may have the necessary finance, idea, and people. Yet, you may not feel ready. It is that moment in sky diving and bungee jumping, when you let go. It is when you are ready to step into the right train knowing what it entails.

You give yourself all of the following reasons and more.

- I am not sure
- I want to think a little more about the idea
- I want to take the views of a few more people
- I want to read up more on entrepreneurship
- I want to prepare myself some more
- Etc., etc.

Here is the thing about entrepreneurship:

- You can never be too sure
- No matter how much you think, your idea will most likely change during execution

- Even if Jeff Bezos personally mentored you, it will not ensure success – you have to test your own destiny
- Most of your training will happen on job

One other thing that is very typical, especially of working professionals - is that they wait for negative circumstances to propel them into change.

A bad boss, a boring job, stagnation, lay-off; these are the usual suspects which push people to an entrepreneurial journey. The trouble with this is two-fold. Firstly, you might be taking the wrong decision which is just driven by circumstances. Secondly, entrepreneurship needs all the positive energy you can garner and more.

> *You are not being fair to yourself, to begin this journey*
> *on a note of bitterness and resentment.*

We are always fascinated by stories of top entrepreneurs who are these Harvard-drop outs. We often read these stories as an example of degrees-don't-matter. But there is another way to see them. All of these ivy-league "drop-outs", like Bill Gates, Elon Musk, left college because their idea was so compelling, that they took the risk of becoming a drop-out. What if their idea had failed miserably? At the time they chose to leave college – failure was an equal possibility. But they took a decision to follow their dreams, leaving a situation which was rosy, a Harvard degree, great job.

> *They left when things were good.*

Not because they were thrown out, or something negative like that. So, don't wait for a bad boss to drive you nuts, so that you think of starting entrepreneurship. Remember our discussion in Chapter II, about why you want to be an entrepreneur. If you are using negative circumstances to launch your entrepreneurship career – then maybe you are running away from your job, rather than running towards entrepreneurship.

Many professionals I know, have all the readiness required to give entrepreneurship a try at this very moment in their lives. Yet they will not take a chance, because things are still not bad at their workplace. They want to milk every ounce out of a job, until they can. In other words, they are waiting for the situation to no longer be good for them, to take a plunge into entrepreneurship. We may not realize that unconsciously we are sending out the wrong signals to the universe, and more importantly, to our own subconscious mind.

- Saying, "let me earn while I can on a job" – is telling yourself I am most likely to be doomed financially once I become an entrepreneur

- Saying, "things are not bad yet, let me continue till the going is good" – is telling yourself, I am not really interested in entrepreneurship, it is just my back-up plan for when I have nothing else to do

- Saying, "I will be a fool to leave my career at a stage I am doing so well – enjoy it while it lasts" is telling yourself that you don't have it in you to repeat your success in another situation

People tell themselves unknowingly, in different ways, that they will fail. They may not realize it, but this is a problem. One thing we know for sure is that entrepreneurship is a mental-game more than anything else. Your mettle gets tested, when the first signs of challenges appear on the horizon. This is where the line gets drawn between those who give up, and those who stay in the game.

> *What we tell our own selves secretly – about whether we will succeed or not, makes all the difference in the end*

So here is what I am saying. If destiny has it, that a terrible experience at work will lead you to think of entrepreneurship, maybe that is your story. But for many others, it is a choice they need to make. If you feel that you have done and accomplished what you had to, and it is time to move on, do so while things are good.

Don't use a negative situation to initiate yourself into something new.

III. Sometimes the right time, is right now

We assume that the opportunity to become an entrepreneur is ever-present, because it's not like someone has to give you a job. "You can do it anytime". That is not true.

Inspiration, mental energy, circumstances will not wait on you for eternity. As they say, time and tide wait for none. Your ideas won't stay relevant forever.

> *You have to board the train, while it is still at the station.*

Many people are also waiting to be at the right time at the right place. But how do you know what is the right time? How can you make sure you are at the right place? I have thought for years about being at the right place at the right time. It is scary at times, and you may wonder – "what if I miss the right time and right place?" Finally, it became clear to me.

> *The moment you decide to do the right thing, is the right time.*

Too much speculation and calculation may not do any good. Even when it comes to entrepreneurship, if you feel reasonably comfortable, go ahead. There is no rule on what is right or wrong. Follow your gut feel.

> *Entrepreneurs are not without fear.*
> *They simply have the ability to find courage.*

It means taking calculated risks. And the meaning of "calculated risk" is that after you have done all the calculations; you have to take the risk.

I wrote a blog recently titled: **"How is life? Well, going on.": why you should NOT quit your job, but GRADUATE from it.**

I wrote it to address the dilemma lot of people face in quitting jobs that are no longer enriching them, forever delaying the decision because of only one reason. Fear.

The perspective I offered in the article was that the fear people experience is largely on the account of seeing "quitting a job" as a one-way move. The assumption is, once you are out, you cannot come back. But what if we saw "doing a job" just as a progression in the continuum of life? We don't stay in school and college forever. We learn, and then graduate. Why can't we similarly, spend time at a regular job, learn, earn and then graduate to the next phase – happily? And just like once in a while we need to go back to college – if needed, we can come back to a job. Can we not look at this transition with a new lens?'

The last point, before the last point, I want to make is this.

The stage of "am I ready to take the plunge" is somewhat like standing at the wedding altar. Sure, everyone feels the jitter. But some, realize at that moment – that this is not for them. That this was just an idea they were fascinated with. But not something they want to live with every moment of their lives. It is like I was telling a friend about my decision to take the plunge into entrepreneurship for the second time. "I am 36 now. I had to tell myself – either I am serious about doing all those grand things I have been dreaming of. Or tell myself to stop bull-shitting". Sometimes, right at the time of taking the plunge, we realize that we have been bull-shitting ourselves. And that's fine. You made a realization. Accept it, instead of making a costly mistake.

However, if you realize entrepreneurship is your true love. Then go ahead, despite the jitters. Making the transition from a job to entrepreneurship, can feel like jumping off a plane for sky diving. And surely, the first few seconds will be as scary as hell. After sometime, hopefully you will start enjoying the feeling of flying in the air. Or you may not; in which case you did prepare for a parachute as a part of your plan. What is sure though, is that you will never know, until you get off the plane. So, that is the final part about evaluating whether or not entrepreneurship is your cup of tea.

> *You will never know... until you are willing to take a sip.*

Reflection guide for Chapter VII

Assessing if you are ready to take the plunge

I. Financial Readiness

1. Do you have saving = 18 months of survival money + initial business expenses?

2. Have you simplified your life-style and spending pattern?

II. Business Readiness

3. Do you have clarity on your idea yet? (i.e. is it more than a vague, "I want to do something on my own")

4. If no, then is it possible for you to have the mind-space, time and energy to get clarity while doing your current job – or are you better off quitting it and creating time and space to figure it out?

5. Do you have some sort of a product prototype ready?

6. If not, is it even possible for you to work on a product idea while being on this job?

7. Are you planning to work on a product which is in competition with your current organization (doing it while on job may create "conflict of interest" issues)?

III. Psychological Readiness

8. Are you doing well in your job – and therefore scared to leave it, while it is still good? (i.e. are you waiting for a time when it will not be so good?)

9. Is the primary reason for you to not take the plunge – fear? (you are giving yourself several excuses)
10. Now that you are at the last step of deciding whether to take the plunge – ask yourself one last tough question – do you really want to become an entrepreneur – or were you merely fascinated by the idea of it?

www.ingramcontent.com/pod-product-compliance
Lightning Source LLC
Chambersburg PA
CBHW020914180526
45163CB00007B/2724